Did you know that
there are single words for . . .

- an excessive dependence on one's mother?
- having a mental block against arithmetic?
- a system of government by the worst citizens?
- someone who never cuts his or her hair?

You'll find all these—and many, many more—in *More Weird Words* . . . another incredible collection of unique, unusual and useful words by the authors of *Weird Words*. *More Weird Words* will give you hours of enjoyment and a vocabulary lesson like one you've never had before!

MORE
WEIRD WORDS

*Berkley Books by Irwin M. Berent and
Rod L. Evans*

WEIRD WORDS
MORE WEIRD WORDS

MORE
WEIRD WORDS

Irwin M. Berent and Rod L. Evans

BERKLEY BOOKS, NEW YORK

MORE WEIRD WORDS

A Berkley Book / published by arrangement with
the authors

PRINTING HISTORY
Berkley edition / July 1995

ISBN: 0-425-14833-5

BERKLEY®
Berkley Books are published by The Berkley Publishing Group,
200 Madison Avenue, New York, New York 10016.
BERKLEY and the "B" design
are trademarks belonging to Berkley Publishing Corporation.

PRINTED IN THE UNITED STATES OF AMERICA

10 9 8 7 6 5 4 3 2 1

Contents

Introduction

In the publishing world, things can happen very fast. No sooner had the original *Weird Words* been released and commenced selling—like the proverbial hotcakes, of course—than our editor was demanding, "More weird words!"

At first we begged him to reconsider. For we knew that when our editor said "more weird words," he really meant "more-weird words"—that is, he wanted not just *more* of the words but words that were *more weird* than before. But how could we possibly succeed at such a task? For *More Weird Words* would have to have even weirder words than those in *Weird Words*. But *are* there words that are actually weirder than "agroof" (flat on one's face), "bibliobibuli" (people who read too much), "echolalus" (one who repeats what he or she hears without comprehending), "geloscopy" (a technique for determining people's character by observing their laughter), "lethologica" (the temporary inability to recall a word or name), or "spanogyny" (scarcity of women), all of which appeared in *Weird Words*?

Well, our editor wouldn't tolerate such logic. And here before you is the result. Mind you, we don't really claim that this collection of weird words is truly weirder than the other one. After all, can very fine degrees of weirdness really be measured? Can one say with certainty that words like "empleomania" (a mania for holding public office), "late-bricole" (hiding or living in holes), and "transvection" (the supernatural conveyance of a witch through the air)—all of which are in this book—are weirder than words like "emacity" (an itch to be buying), "lassipedes" (tired feet), and "tropophobia" (fear of making changes)—all of which are in the other book? So you can see why the title of this book is *More Weird Words,* not *More-Weird Words.*

But whether the words in this book are weirder or just weird, we believe they're weird enough. Alas, though, weirdness is not a permanent state, at least where words are concerned. We can remember a time not so long ago—in fact, just a few months ago—when readers of *Weird Words* thought "exungulate" and "infucate" were weird. Now all we hear is that "He's exungulating" (trimming his nails) or that "She's infucating" (putting on makeup). People have used the words they read in *Weird Words* so often that they—the words, that is—just don't seem as weird as they used to seem. The trouble is that once you get to know weird things—like those words (and some people)—they don't seem all that weird any longer.

The big secret, then, is that words are weird only when rarely used. Once they're used by everyone, they're just useful—and that's exactly what we want these words to be: used. So please, go on and use them; that's what weird words are for.

And remember, these words won't be weird forever, so get 'em while they're hot!

What Good Are
One-of-a-Kind Words?

It's a funny thing, the English language. We have perhaps over a million words from which to choose. And each word has its own charm and beauty, its own color and texture, so that if one word is not precisely suitable or does not express the precise idea or feeling, there is almost always another word that will, the variety in our language being so great. There are in fact so many words that no single dictionary can contain all of them, and yet—here's the irony—we often can't find a good word with which to express ourselves.

A result is that we have even come to think that there *are* no words to denote a number of quite common situations and issues. For example, how many people know that there actually is a single word for "swallowing food without chewing" or for "seeking an inheritance" or for "being full of beer"?

Well, believe it or not, there *is* a single word for each of those phrases—a fact that shouldn't surprise you too much if you've read *Weird Words*. Those words are, in the same order, "psomophagy," "heredipety," and "gambrinous." Such words are unique, in that they are essentially the only words that denote precisely those three things.

In other words, they have no synonyms. We've coined the word "insynonymable" (insinuhNIMable) to describe a word that has no synonyms. In effect, you will not find any word in this book whose meaning could be conveyed by any other single well-known word. For example, "cunctatious" would require at least three other words—"addicted to delaying"—to express the same idea; there is no common one-word synonym for "cunctatious." You could, of course, use the word "procrastinating," but it would not adequately capture the meaning of "cunctatious."

This dictionary contains some of the most fascinating words in the English language, many of which are insynonymable and most of which have, until now, been remarkably difficult to find. In addition, the ThesauroIndex, designed especially for this dictionary, helps make these words easy to find. (To learn how to get the most use from the ThesauroIndex, see "How to Use this Book.")

How Should You Use Rare Words?

You're probably thinking now, "But if these words have been so difficult to find, and if, therefore, few people know their meanings, how can I use the words without utterly baffling the person to whom I'm speaking or writing?"

Of course, some of you may *like* to baffle others, either because you want to show people that you know something that they don't or because you want them to suspect— incorrectly—that they have been insulted. For example, to someone who has just complained about someone else's smoking, you might say, "What are you, some kind of misocapnist?" Doubtless, though, your "victims" will be sufficiently puzzled or provoked simply to ask you what "misocapnist" means. And at that point you can choose either to enlighten them ("It means 'one who hates tobacco smoke'") or leave them steaming.

There are, however, less sadistic and pompous ways to make effective use of rare words. The fact is, you can use rare words so that they require virtually no explanation to be understood. Consider, for example, this sentence in which it is reasonably obvious that the word "kakistocracy" probably relates to government by the worst citizens: "This government is closer to a kakistocracy than a democracy, since it is run by the worst rulers."

You can also use the words instructively, as when you say or write: "You must have gotten up on the wrong side of the bed this morning; in other words, you've got matutolypea." Note that the word order—that is, the syntax—in that sentence is less likely to be interpreted as condescending than the reverse order: "You've got matutolypea—that is, a tendency to get up on the wrong side of the bed." If the person to whom you're speaking already knows what that word means, the sentence might sound condescending.

At times, the physical surroundings will provide enough clues to enable your listener to grasp your meaning quite clearly. For example, as you hand someone a can of underarm deodorant, while holding your nose with your other hand, you might say, "Perhaps this will help you with your tragomaschalia."

Finally, if your listener is still baffled, there is always the following alternative—a special favorite of ours, for obvious reasons: "Look it up in Berent and Evans." Indeed, once this book becomes a best-seller, many of its words might fall into common usage, and soon everyone will be using them. (Hey, we can dream, can't we?)

Why Aren't These Words Used More Often?

Perhaps one reason why many of the words in this dictionary have not fallen into common use is that their usefulness is often not readily apparent. But the words here have been selected not merely because they are unique but also because they lend themselves to figurative as well as literal use. In other words, some of these words may have only very narrow usefulness when they're used literally. The word "disgorger," for example, can be used literally only to denote the actual instrument (a disgorger) used to remove a hook from the mouth of a fish. But even though its literal use is limited, imaginative writers and speakers can come up with a number of quite colorful and illustrative figurative uses for a word like "disgorger." If you were writing about someone who fell for some scam—who, as they say, "took the bait"—you might say that the person now "needs a disgorger" to get out of the situation.

Or consider the word "dextrovert," which means "to turn to the right." Although it's a useful word to designate a direction, it can also easily be converted to political use: "Although American politics moved toward the left in the 1960s and 1970s, former President Reagan effected a political dextroversion in the 1980s."

Numerous other words can be used figuratively, too. For example, "remontant" (flowering more than once in a season) could pertain to anything that happens regularly more than once each year, and "hemianopsia" (a condition of half or partial blindness) can be applied to one who understands only a part of something, and so on.

Taken as a whole, the words in this dictionary should make for entertaining reading. You may, for example, be delightfully surprised at times to find words that denote things for which you would have doubted there were words.

For example, "ucalegon" (a neighbor whose house is on fire) is a great word when applied figuratively to neighboring nations with major domestic problems.

More Weird Words should be as useful to writers as it will be entertaining to word-lovers—logophiles, that is. Open it anywhere and enjoy!

How to Use This Book

You can use this dictionary in two main ways. One is simply to pick it up and start reading. At almost any page you may find a number of fascinating words that you never knew existed. If, however, you want to find a word for a specific subject, you'll want first to use the ThesauroIndex, located at the back of this book.

Using the ThesauroIndex

Think of a word that generally pertains to the subject in which you're interested, and then look up that topic word in the ThesauroIndex. There you'll find a list of specific words to which to refer in the dictionary, or you'll be directed to see another topic word instead.

For example, if you want to find words related to pimples, you'll look up "pimples" and find two words— "horripilation" and "phaneromania"—listed under that topic. You can then look up those two words in the main dictionary. If you had looked under, say, "blemishes" rather than "pimples," the ThesauroIndex would have told you to see "pimples."

Suppose, however, that after looking up "horripilation" and "phaneromania," you find that neither word is quite the one you need. You can now use the ThesauroIndex much as you would use an ordinary thesaurus, for under each topic

8

word, you'll find a list of related categories to consult. In the present example, you would return to the ThesauroIndex topic word, "pimples," and find the following:

PIMPLES (see also BEAUTY, GROWTH/DEFORMITY, MAKEUP, SPOTS, WOUNDS, WRINKLES)
    horripilation, phaneromania

You can then consult each of those related topics as well, or just consult one or a few of them. Suppose you decide, for example, that "makeup" might be a useful topic. You look it up in the ThesauroIndex and then consult the words listed under that topic. Still not satisfied? Then return to the "makeup" topic and see what related topics are suggested.

MAKEUP (see also BEAUTY, CHARACTER, COVER-ING, WRINKLES)
    fard, infucation

Some of the topics suggested are the same as those suggested under "pimples," but some are new: "Character" and "Covering." The more topics you consult, the deeper you will get into the shades and colors of meaning of the original idea for which you were searching. Thus, starting with words related to pimples, you may end up with "beauism" (the tendency to give excessive attention to matters of dress and etiquette), which is listed with several other words under the topic "covering."

So by using the ThesauroIndex you may discover a whole universe of ideas and senses that your original word only begins to capture. Indeed, every topic word is followed by at least one cross-reference to another topic word, and some more general topic words carry ten or more cross-references. This means you can begin with only the vaguest

9

idea of the word you're seeking and be led to the most nearly precise and most colorful word for your needs. Often, in fact, a cross-reference is made to a figuratively related heading. For example, "mountains" carries a cross-reference to "problems." In the end, the word that you arrive at may represent anything from an exact denotation of a concrete object to a word that conveys a humorous figurative idea.

Some Notes about the Definitions

Note that we do not usually specify whether a word is an adjective, noun, verb, or adverb. Remember that most definitions beginning with an *-ing* or *-ed* word are definitions of adjectives (at least, this is true for this dictionary); those beginning with "a," "the," "one who," or a *-tion* word are usually definitions of nouns; those beginning with "to" are verbs; and those beginning with "by," "for," "with," and so on are adverbs.

Note also that we have not always given all the possible definitions for each word entered but only those definitions or parts of definitions that are most colorful, useful, and unusual.

A Note on Pronunciation and Word Origins

We've included the pronunciations of all headwords whose pronunciations might otherwise be in doubt. We've also explained the roots of many headwords, especially those that are unusual or otherwise interesting.

We have provided only a brief explanation of the meanings and origins of the roots, however, not a detailed etymological analysis. Where a related word is defined within one of these root explanations, we have given only a partial definition that is immediately pertinent to the root in question. Finally, where an ancient or Indo-European root is presented, keep in mind that these ultimate, or original, roots are very often based on speculation—that is, etymologists have concluded that a root pronounced roughly a certain way is most likely the source of a particular word. In almost every instance, of course, this original word preceded written history and has therefore not been found.

CAPitalized LETters INdicate ACcented PORtion of word

ā = late	bird /	s = sit
a = pat	turn	sh = show
aw = **aw**e / b**a**r /	g = get	th = thin
b**ough**t	ī = bike	*th* = the
ch = child	i = pit	u = but / pull
ch = German	j = joy	*u* = boot
"ch"	ō = rope	' = very short
ē = Pete	o = pot	"uh"
e = pet	*oi* = oil / boy	• = for pause
er = wat**er** /	*ow* = out / cow	or clarification
w**or**d /	*or* = bore /	
	tour	

Dictionary

A

absquatulate (absKWOch*u* • lāt)   to leave hurriedly, suddenly, or secretly

"The extortionists must be tracked down, since they have **absquatulated** with the money."

abulia (āBY*U*lēu)   loss of willpower

"You must guard against **abulia** if you wish to give up smoking or any other destructive habit."

acalculia (ākalKY*U*lēu)   the inability to work with numbers; a mental block against arithmetic

"The man who bounced the check explained to his banker that he was unable to balance his checkbook because he had **acalculia**."

"Acalculia" (literally, not calculating) comes from the same original root as such words as "calcium," "chalk," and "calculus." What all these words have in common is stone: calcium deposits are like stone; chalk is composed of limestone; and a calculus is a concretion, sometimes found in the body. But what, you may ask, do stones have to do with calculating? Stones, as you may have guessed, were once used for counting. They were our first true calculators.

acatalepsy (āKADulepsē) state of being impossible to understand

"Because she believes that absolute knowledge is an ideal impossible to realize, she subscribes to a doctrine of **acatalepsy**."

aceldama (uSELdumu) field or scene of bloodshed

"Many Civil War soldiers couldn't believe the horror of the **aceldama**."

acersecomic (ASer • suKOMik) one whose hair has never been cut

"She would have been an **acersecomic** had she not been married to a barber who insisted that she get a haircut now and then."

acetarious (asuTARēus) pertaining to plants used in salads

"Please remove this rutabaga from the salad, since rutabagas, unlike carrots, are not **acetarious**."

achromatopsia (ĀkrōmuTOPsēu), **daltonism** color-blindness

"We knew she had **achromatopsia** when she couldn't discern the colored letters in the eye test."

14

Top is *not* one of the roots in "achromatopsia." Its three roots are *a* (not), *chromat* (color), and *opsia* (sight).

Daltonism is named for John Dalton (1766–1844), who presented in 1794 a systematic account of color-blindness and who was himself color-blind.

achthronym (AKthrunim), **ethnophaulism** (ethnōF*AW*liz′m) an ethnic slur

> "The comedian's sexist jokes and **achthronyms** soon ended his career."

acouasm (aK*U*uz′m) an imagined ringing in the ear

> "Is that the doorbell or merely my **acouasm**?"

acrolect (AKrulekt) the most prestigious dialect in a language

> "The Cockney knew he wasn't speaking an **acrolect**."

acromegalic (AKrō • meGALik) having oversized arms and legs or excessive growth

> "Either the baby has been working out, or she's just naturally **acromegalic**."

acronyx (AKrōniks) an ingrowing toenail

> "To make sure your **acronyx** doesn't grow back, we'll need to remove part of the nail's root."

aculeate (akY*U*lēut) equipped with a sting; an insect with a sting

"Since bees are **aculeate** insects, I recommend that you avoid dressing like a flower if you want to avoid being stung."

The *ac* is the important root in this word. *Ak* is the ancient Indo-European root meaning "sharp" or "pointed." A point, of course, may be a needle, which can sting. In another sense, a point's sharpness may apply to a sharp or sour taste—hence "**ac**idic" and "**ac**rid." And a point is often the end or top of something—hence the **Ac**ropolis was literally the city on the hill, and **ac**robats jump high in the air. And sometimes a point is located on the "**edge**." (See also "**oxy**moron.")

adiaphoristic   (adē • afuRIStik)   theologically indifferent

"They were criticized for being **adiaphoristic** during doctrinal disputes."

adiathermic   (adēuTHER mik)   impervious to heat

"In a sense, Reagan was the **adiathermic** president, since no amount of heat from the press could shake his image."

admanuensis   (admany*u*ENsis)   one who takes an oath by touching the Bible

"Even a nonbeliever usually becomes an **admanuensis** before he or she takes the stand in court."

admass   (admas)   pertaining to those people who are susceptible to the persuasion of the mass media, especially publicity and advertising

"She buys products only when she knows they are reliable, because she is not gullible and not vulnerable to **admass** manipulation."

adnascent (adNASent) growing on something else

"Like a tumor, fear can be both **adnascent** and destructive, though it grows in the mind rather than in the body."

Adonis (uDONis) a handsome man

"Cary Grant was widely considered an **Adonis**."

adoxography (adoksOGrufē) writing cleverly on a trivial subject

"Charles Lamb's humorous essay, 'A Dissertation on Roast Pig,' is a good example of **adoxography**."

Doxography is the collecting and compiling of, and commenting on, writings of ancient Greek philosophers. When the prefix *a-* (not) is added to "doxography," the word pertains, in effect, to writings that are not as important as Greek philosophy, but that are presented as though they are.

The *dox* part of this word comes from the Indo-European root *dek* (to take, to accept). Thus, that which is acceptable is **dec**ent; that which is worthy of acceptance is related to "**dign**ified," "**dec**orous," and "**dain**ty" (from the Latin "**dign**itas"); that which causes people to accept certain things or beliefs is embodied in a number of words, including "**doc**tor," "**doc**trine," "**doc**ument," "ortho**dox**y,"

17

and "**dog**ma." And indeed, philosophers and commentators do try to get others to accept their points of view.

agathokakological   (AGuthō • kakuLOJuk'l)   composed of both good and evil

"The minister held that none of us parishioners was completely good or bad, but every one of us is **agathokakological**."

agelast   (Ajilast)   one who never laughs

"Don't rely on **agelasts** for sympathy, since those who don't laugh won't be able to cheer you up."

agenocratia   (uJENōKRATēu)   opposition to birth control

"Their **agenocratia** is rooted in their religious conviction that to practice birth control is to thwart the natural function of one's organs."

ageotropic   (ujēuTROPik)   turning away from the earth

"The minister held that our efforts must be **ageotropic** and heavenward."

agerasia   (ajuRĀsēu)   youthful appearance in an older person

"Always known for his **agerasia**, Dick Clark looks almost as young now as he did thirty years ago."

Members of the geriatric set are older people. So "agerasia" is literally "not" (*a*) "old age" (*geras*).

ageusia (uGY*U*zēu) loss of or damage to the sense of taste

"While she was afflicted with **ageusia**, she didn't care what she ate."

agiotage (Ajudij) stock speculation

"**Agiotage** is a form of gambling, but it's done with stocks."

The *agio* part of this word is related in an interesting, roundabout way to the common word "else." *Agio* relates to the exchange of money—in other words, getting one thing for another thing (something else). *Agio* comes from the Italian *aggio*, which in turn comes from Italian dialect *lajje*. And *lajje* comes from the Middle Greek *allagion* (meaning "exchange") and the Greek *allage* (change). Finally and ultimately, the Greek word comes from the Greek *allos* (other), from which the word "else" comes directly.

What, though, happened to the *all* part? Why did the Middle Greek *allagion* become simply *aggio* in Italian? Well, first, in Italian dialect, the *a* wasn't pronounced. Result: *lajje*. Then, the *l* was mistakenly assumed to be an article, like "el" in Spanish or "the" or "an" in English, and was therefore dropped. The error is similar to that made by one who mistakes "theater" for "the ater," assuming that the "the" in "theater" is an article rather than an actual part of the word "theater."

aichmophobia (īkmōF*Ō*bēu) fear of needles and other pointed objects

"Since his **aichmophobia** extended to knitting needles, we hid them when he was around."

ailurophile   (īLERufīl)   a cat lover

"She was an **ailurophile** and felt driven to take in more than a dozen stray cats."

ailurophobe   (īLerufōb)   one who has a morbid fear of cats

"He was such an **ailurophobe** that he couldn't stay in the same room with a cat without breaking out in a nervous sweat."

akimbo   (uKIMbō)   with hands on hips

"With his arms **akimbo**, the drill sergeant seemed even more intimidating than usual."

alalia   (āLĀlēu), **aphasia** (uFĀZyu)   loss of speech

"Her brain lesion resulted in **alalia**, which often discouraged her from even trying to talk."

albescent   (alBESunt)   growing white, as hair

"His **albescent** hair made him look distinguished, at least to many people."

The *alb* part of this word means "white." It appears also in "**alb**ino," "**alb**umen," (the white of the egg), and "**alb**um" (having blank, and originally white, pages). "**Aub**urn," though it denotes reddish-brown hair, also originates from "**alb**urnus," meaning "whitish." At some point, "auburn," sounding similar to "brown," acquired its current meaning. (See also "d**aub**.")

aleatory (ĀLēutorē)   depending on chance or luck

"Her success, like that of most people, was a result of a combination of diligent work and **aleatory** factors, such as loving, encouraging parents."

alexia (uLEKsēu)   inability to read

"Listening to audio tapes of books is especially useful for those who have **alexia**."

amblysia (amBLIZyu)   phrasing intended to cushion bad news, but sometimes alarming in itself, as when one begins with, "Now, I don't want to alarm you, but . . ."

"When he prefaced his remarks by saying, 'I don't like to present bad news, but . . .' we knew that he was engaging in **amblysia**."

amicicide (aMIKisīd)   the killing of a friend

"Even though they have known each other for twenty years, neither greedy man would shrink from **amicicide** for the right price."

The *amic* part of this word is, as you may have guessed, the same root found in some other words related to friendship and friendliness, especially "**amic**able" and "**ami**able." Actually, the Latin root of those words is *amare* or *amatum*, each of which means "love." Hence, an **ama**teur plays for the love of the sport; en**em**ies are those who are not loved; and **amor**ous behavior is engaged by someone in love.

Interestingly, the *am* parts of all those words originate from the Indo-European word *amma*, for the person we all love: *Momma*! "Mama" is simply baby talk and the sound of suckling. From that root we have "**mot**her," "**mat**ernity," "**met**ropolis" (mother city), and even "**ma**tter."

anabiosis (anubiŌsis) returning to life after seeming death

"In the book *Life after Life*, the author documents out-of-body reports, which are supposed to be describing **anabioses**."

anacampserote (anuKAMP*ser*ōt) something that can bring back a lost love

"The scientist held that there are no **anacampserotes**, since the dead do not return."

anachorism (anAK*eriz*′m) something foreign or not suited to a country; something geographically impossible or absurd

"Expecting democracy to be easily absorbed into the minds and hearts of people who have known only tyranny and have demanded nothing else is expecting a nation to adopt an **anachorism**."

anaclitic (anuKLITik) in psychology, being excessively dependent on the mother

"The **anaclitic** young man constantly felt obliged to ask his mother for permission."

anacoenosis (anusēNŌSis) a request for another's opinion

"Since wise leaders know that they don't have all the answers, they engage in **anacoenosis** to get expert advice."

anhedonia (anhēDŌNēu)   the inability to experience pleasure

"A person who has **anhedonia** doesn't take pleasure in even those activities that he or she usually likes."

Hedone is the Greek word for "pleasure," from which arises our word "hedonist" and other *hedo* words. The original root is from the Indo-European *suad*, meaning "sweet" or "pleasant." The *suad* root gave rise not only to the Greek *hedone* but also to the Latin *suadere*, which in turn gave root to the English words "**swe**et" and "per-**suad**e"—by offering sweet talk, one can often successfully persuade!

At first glance, the Latin *suadere* and the Greek *hedone* do not appear to be related, since one begins with an *s* and the other with an *h*. Keep in mind, though, that a number of Latin roots beginning with *s* have the same meanings as Greek roots beginning with *h*. For example, both *septa-* (Latin origin) and *hepta-* (Greek origin) mean "seven," and both *somno-* (Latin) and *hypno-* (Greek) mean "sleep."

aniconic (anīKONik)   not using or permitting images, effigies, or idols

"Because ancient Judaism was an **aniconic** religion, the archaeologists knew they wouldn't discover a great deal of art in that society."

anomie, anomy (Anumē)   a situation in which a society is not governed by the norms that generally regulate behavior; an absence of law, or an absence of regard for law, especially natural law.

"During the French Revolution, French society temporarily fell into **anomie**."

"The thoroughly naturalistic philosopher held that the universe operates only according to scientific laws, which make any miracle an example of **anomie** and hence an impossibility."

anopisthographic (ANu • pisthuGRAFik) bearing writing, or printing on one side only

"Except for signatures, checks are **anopisthographic**."

anosmia (aNOSmēu) loss of the sense of smell

"Those people who work down in the sewer are fortunate if they have **anosmia**; otherwise, they must bear the smell or quit."

The *osm* part of this word is from the Greek word for "smell," *osmein*, which in turn comes from the Indo-European root, *od*, also meaning "smell." A few other English words have *osm* in them, though perhaps the best-known *osm* word, "osmosis," is in fact *not* related to those "smell" words.

From the *od* and *osm* roots we ultimately get our word for a pungent form of oxygen, "**oz**one."

The Latin, and in turn English, word "**od**or" also originates from the *od* root. So too does the Latin word *olere*, meaning "smell." From that word we have, for example, "**ol**factory" (pertaining to the sense of smell) and "red**ol**ent" (scented, aromatic; evocative).

antapology   (antuPOLujē)   the reply to an apology, as in saying "That's all right" after someone has apologized for stepping on your foot

   "When she responded to my apology by smiling and saying 'No problem,' I greeted her **antapology** with a relieved grin."

antephialtic   (antefēALtik)   preventive of nightmares

   "After seeing the original movie *Nightmare on Elm Street*, his daughter thought that her teddy bear might be **antephialtic**."

anthropopithecus   (anthru•popiTHĒkus)   hypothetical animal thought of as the missing link

   "I would be too kind if I said the visitor was ill-mannered; he may actually be **anthropopithecus**—in person."

antinomian   (antuNOmēun)   Christian who believes that faith alone will secure salvation

   "She isn't an **antinomian**: she believes that good works are required of all people."

antisyzygy   (antiSIZijē)   a union of opposites

   "When the conservative Wordsworth joined forces with the nonconformist Coleridge for the writing of

Lyrical Ballads, they formed an **antisyzygy** for which we are still appreciative."

This peculiar-looking word is composed of three main roots: *anti, sy* (or *syn*), and *zyg*. The *zyg* root, by far the most unusual of the three roots, is actually related to a number of everyday English words. The *zyg* originated in the Indo-European root *ieug* (or *ius*), meaning "join together, unite," and, in an extended sense, "shake together, mix." Hence, English has the words "**juice**" (mixed substances), "**yoke**" (from Sanskrit *yuga*), "**zyg**ote" (a union of gametes, from Greek *zygon*, meaning "yoke" or "pair"), "**enzyme**" (used for fermenting; hence, from Greek *zume*, meaning "ferment"), "**jux**tapose" (from Latin *juxta*, meaning "near"), and "**junc**tion" (from Latin *jungere*, meaning "to join").

antiverbality   (ANti • *ver*BALitē)   a disinclination or outright distaste for using speech to communicate

"President Calvin Coolidge was known for his **antiverbality**."

anuptaphobia   (uNUPtuFŌbēu)   fear of staying single

"Because of his **anuptaphobia**, he remarried two weeks after his divorce."

For information about the *nup* part of this word, see "nympholepsy."

apaetesis   (apuTĒsis)   the act of angrily putting aside a matter for later discussion, as when one says, "Forget it! We'll talk about it later!"

"She resented her husband's **apaetesis**, since she wanted to discuss the matter then and there."

aporia (uP*OR*ēu) the expression of a doubt, real or feigned, about where to begin, what to say, or how to express something

"The hesitant and disjointed remarks of his **aporia** testified to his uncertainty about how to express his feelings."

The *por* in this word is a very common root in the language. It is related to a *per/por/fer/for* root meaning "carrying" or "passing through." For example, "trans**port**," "**por**e" (a minute opening or passageway), "em**por**ium" (from Greek **por**os, meaning "thoroughfare," hence "a trading place" or "marketplace"), "thorough**fare**," "**fare**" (money required to pass through), "**fer**ry," and even "s**port**" (from "des**por**ter," meaning "carry apart," the idea being that one gets "carried away" from more serious activities when engaged in sport).

aposiopesis (apusīuPĒsis) breaking off in the middle of a statement, often out of embarrassment or concern that what you were going to say might be offensive: "You really surprised me when you . . . well, I'd better not say it."

"He held back his potentially insulting remark at the last possible moment with a perfectly timed **aposiopesis**."

apostil (uPOStil) a note written in the margin

"The teacher added an **apostil** to explain why she disagreed with the student's statement in the first part of the essay."

apotropaic (aputruPĀik)   having the power to ward off evil

"The professor rejected as useless the rabbit's foot, the horseshoe, the amulet, and all other allegedly **apotropaic** objects."

aprosexia (āprōSEKSēu)   inability to concentrate

"Every time I'm distracted by an attractive woman, **aprosexia** takes over, so that I'm unable to concentrate."

Don't be fooled by the *sex* part of this word—it's one of those purely accidental creations in the language. The *exia* part comes from the Greek word *echein* (to hold); the *pros* part means "toward"; and the *a* means "not." So the whole word translates roughly as "not holding toward," or "not turning (one's attention) to."

The word "eunuch" also comes from the Greek *echein*: *eun* derives from the Greek word for "bed," and *uch* comes from *echein* (to hold). Hence, a eunuch, having been castrated, was an appropriate person to hold—or keep or watch over—the bedchamber of one's harem. (So we managed to get into sex after all, didn't we?)

apteryx (APturiks)   a flightless bird, such as the penguin

"Without funding for its engines, the massive state-of-the-art spaceship was a powerless **apteryx**."

The *pt* in "**a**pteryx" is the important part. Numerous words with *p* and *t* near each other are related, all going back to an ancient root, *pet* (rush, leap, fly, fall). From that root, we get "helico**pter**" (*heliko* plus *pteron*, meaning "helix" plus "wing, feather"), "**pter**odactyl" (wing-fingered reptile), "**pt**omaine" (fallen body), "sym**pt**om" (literally, a falling together), "asym**pt**ote" (not falling together), "hippo**pot**amus" (river horse: *potamus* is "river," which is, of course, flowing water). And since *p* and *f* are closely related linguistically, the word "**feather**" is, not surprisingly, related too.

Finally, from the related Latin word, *petere*, meaning "go forward," or "seek," we get such words as "com**pete**," "**pet**ition," "centri**pet**al," and "ap**pet**ite."

ascian (ASH[ē]un) one without a shadow

"I know that vampires are not reflected in mirrors, but I'm not sure whether they are also **ascians**."

aseity (āSĒutē) absolute independence (often used in referring to God)

"According to the theologian, everything finite depends on God, but God depends on nothing else and therefore enjoys perfect **aseity**."

"Aseity" comes directly from the Latin phrase, *a se*, meaning "from (*a* or *ab*) oneself," the idea being that one is completely self-sufficient, getting everything from oneself. The *se* root ultimately comes from the Indo-European word for "self": *se* (or *swe* or *sue*). From that root we have "**sui**cide" (killing oneself) and "**si**bling" (literally, one's own relative) as well as the word "**se**lf" itself.

In addition, we have words that relate to separateness, in the sense of being "to oneself" or "apart": "**se**parate," "**se**cret" (kept from everyone else), "**se**duce" (drawing one

29

away), and so on. Even the word "ethics" (the basic moral character that makes oneself) comes from the Indo-European root *sue-do*, meaning literally "self do" or "self make." The *su* part of *suedo* was later dropped.

asonia (aSŌNēu)   inability to distinguish among different pitches

   "People with **asonia** should not be asked to sing 'The Star-Spangled Banner' in front of millions of baseball fans."

asphalia (asfuLĪu)   the guaranteeing of what one is saying, as when one prefaces a statement with, "I can *assure* you that . . ." or "I'll wager my last dollar that . . ."

   "We weren't convinced by the coach's **asphalia**, only by his track record."

asteism (AStēiz'm)   an ingeniously polite insult

   "She's so skilled at **asteism** that a compliment from her may well be a subtle jab."

asymptotically (asim[p]TOTiklē)   getting closer but never quite meeting

   "Although we can approximate those ideals only **asymptotically**, they are excellent guides."

B

backberend (BAKberund) a thief caught with the stolen goods

"Our burglar alarm enabled us to catch the **backberend** red-handed."

Balkanize (BAWLkunīz) to split up a region into small, weak, and frequently conflicting states

"Serbs and Croats know exactly what it means for a country to be **Balkanized** into warring factions."

This word comes from the name of the Balkan Peninsula, which was divided into several small nations in the early twentieth century.

ballistophobia (buLISTuFŌbēu) fear of being shot

"His **ballistophobia** was so severe that he would never go to the post office for fear of being shot by a disgruntled employee."

banality (bāNALutē) an insipid or obvious remark

"After Calvin Coolidge said that when people lose their jobs unemployment results, he spoke what was to become a famous **banality**."

banderilla (banduRĒu) a barbed, decorated dart used by banderillos in bullfighting

"His subtle comment, like a **banderilla**, was colorful, but painful nonetheless."

bandwagon fallacy (BANDwagun FALusē) the fallacy of arguing that an idea or practice is acceptable because it's popular

"When people argue that I should prefer a soft drink because it is leading in the cola wars, I know that they've committed the **bandwagon fallacy**."

banshee (BANshē) spirit heralding death

"As soon as the soldiers fell into the trap, they probably heard the shrieks of the **banshee**."

bantingism (BANtingiz'm) dieting by avoiding sweets

"**Bantingism** isn't enough; you must not only avoid sweets but also eat fruits and vegetables if you want to lose weight and stay well."

baragnosis (baragNŌSis) lack or loss of the ability to judge the weight of an object

"The corrupt grocery merchant pretended that his practice of overcharging his customers for luncheon meats was due to **baragnosis**, not dishonesty."

"Baragnosis" is literally "weight" (*bar*) plus "not" (*a*) plus "knowing" (*gnosis*). A person with baragnosis has lost bar*o*gnosis (with an *o*), perception of weight by the cutaneous and muscle senses.

The *bar* in "baragnosis" come from the Greek *bruein*, meaning "swell." That which is swollen is indeed heavy— weighty, that is. From that root we also get "em**bryo**," (a swelling within), "**bru**te," the deep-voiced, heavy "**bari**tone," and "**bar**ometer," the instrument that measures barometric pressure.

batten   (BATun)   to live well at another's expense

"In theory, politicians are expected to serve the taxpayers, not **batten** on them."

battologist   (baTOLujist)   one who pointlessly repeats himself.

"The wife accused her husband of being a **battologist** because each day he would say the same thing: 'We can't afford it.' "

beauism   (BŌiz'm)   the tendency to give excessive attention to matters of dress and etiquette

"Dressed a bit too well and knowing little, the new senator was more dedicated to **beauism** than to public service."

bellipotent   (beLIPutent)   powerful in war

"If this country is to survive, it needs to be **bellipotent** as well as economically powerful."

The *belli* part of this word comes from the Classical Latin *bellum*, meaning "war." This root also appears in "**bellig**-erent," "**belli**cose" (warlike), and "ante**bellum**" (before the [Civil] war). "Duel" also comes from *bellum*: the archaic Latin word for "war"—*duellum*—became *bellum* in Classical Latin, in accordance with the trend in early Latin to change *du*, when it preceded a vowel, to *b*.

bellwether (BELwe*ther*) the leader of a sheeplike and foolish crowd.

"The corrupt televangelist used to be one of the principal **bellwethers** of the religious right."

belvedere (BELvud**ē**r) a building overlooking a fine view

"The hotel was a marvelous **belvedere**, since from every window there was a breathtaking sight to behold."

benedict (BENudikt) a newly married man

"After the wedding the groom looked confused by his new stature as a **benedict**."

bimester (B**Ī**Mes*ter*) a two-month period

"She would spend June and July on vacation and then spend another **bimester** writing her articles."

binal (B**Ī**n′l) two by two

"Many of Noah's animals entered his ark in a **binal** formation."

biophillism (bīOFuliz′m) the belief that animals have rights that human beings should respect

"After reading the book *Animal Liberation*, some people became passionate **biophillists**."

The main roots of this word are *bio* (life) and *phil* (love). Interestingly and perhaps ironically, a word with the same roots, "bio**phil**ous," means "parasitic." Indeed, one who loves living things can respect them *or* exploit them.

birl (b*e*rl) to revolve a log in the water while standing on it

"Teaching at the university was like trying to **birl**; I stood on one end of the log, while the dean stood at the other, disagreeing with every proposal I made."

biunial (bīyUnēul) combining two in one

"The adverisement made the claim that the **biunial** product was both a breath mint and a candy—in short, 'two mints in one.'"

blabagogy (BLABugojē) criminal environment

"The gang members were describing the **blabagogy** in which they grew up."

bletonism (BLETuniz′m) the alleged ability to perceive an underground water supply

"With her divining rod she claimed to have powers of **bletonism**."

blinkard (BLINK*erd*)   someone who ignores or avoids something

"Many people have accused members of congress of being **blinkards** who, they claim, did nothing to prevent or diminish the savings and loan crisis."

Also an archaic word for one who blinks a lot, "blinkard" originates from a root that actually meant not a closing but an *opening* of the eyes. "Blink" comes from the Indo-European root *bhel* (shine, brightness, blaze). That root has ultimately given us "**bal**d" (shiny head), "**bl**each," "**bl**ond," "**bl**ank" (originally meant "white, not written on"), and "**bl**anket" (originally "a white material").

bouffage (b*u*FOZH)   a satisfying meal

"The fraternity boy rubbed his stomach and smiled as he gulped down the last of his **bouffage**."

brackish (BRAKi*sh*)   having an unpleasant salty taste

"The smoked fish was unfortunately **brackish**."

bradyauxesis (BRADē·*aw*gZĒsis)   in an organism, the growth of one part at a slower rate than the whole

"Our biology teacher made fun of our star football player by saying that he illustrated the phenomenon of **bradyauxesis**, since his brain was apparently developing far more slowly than the rest of his body."

"Auxesis" (in biology, an increase in size without division of the cell) originates from an Indo-European root for "increase": *aug*. *Aug* (and *augs*—hence, *aux*) has given us "**aug**ment," "**aux**iliary," "**auth**or" (from Middle English "auctour," meaning "originator"—in a sense, "a grower of words and ideas"), "**auc**tion" (in which bidding goes higher and higher), "**aug**ust" (majestic, in a sense representing a great increase), and "in**aug**urate."

In German, **aug** became **eke** (*g* and *k* are related in pronunciation), which ultimately gave us the verb "wax" (to increase in size, strength, or intensity), and, believe it or not, "nickname," which was originally two words: "an **eke**name"—that is, an additional (increased) name.

bradycardia (BRAduK*AW*Rdēu) slow heart rate

"The athlete said that his **bradycardia** was a product of years of training."

bradytelic (BRAdiTELik) having a slower than normal rate of evolution

"The author H. L. Mencken contemptuously regarded extremely conservative Christians as **bradytelic**."

C

cachinnate (KAKināt) to laugh noisily or immoderately

"Kathleen was nicknamed 'Cackleleen' because of her tendency to **cachinnate**."

cacographer (kaKOGruf*er*) one who spells or writes badly

"Even excellent writers can have trouble spelling, as **cacographer** F. Scott Fitzgerald could have testified."

Like the other entries with the *kaka* sound—"*kaki*drosis," "*kaki*stocracy," "*kako*rrhaphiophobia," and so on—"*caco*grapher" has a root originating from baby talk for "feces": *cacca*. *Cacca* has produced several compound words that relate to badness, including, for example, "**caco**phony," and "**co**prolite" (fossilized excrement; the *ka* sound is not repeated), and even "poppy**cock**." (See also "Kalli**kak**" and "agatho**kak**ological.")

cacophonophilist (kaKOFuNOFulist) a lover of harsh sounds

"Our music critic, who considers rock and roll strident junk, believes that it will continue to make money because it appeals to millions of **cacophonophilists**."

caducity (kuDYUsutē) weakness due to old age

"Although she was vital and strong when she was young, her **caducity** prevented her from lifting even light objects when she grew old."

cafard (KOfor) French slang term for the madness produced by terminal boredom

"After years of constant idleness, he fell victim to **cafard** and so was beyond reason."

cagamosis (kaguMŌsis) an unhappy marriage

"If people chose their marriage partners more carefully and were more willing to compromise and respect differences, we'd have few **cagamoses**."

calathus (KALuthus), **calathos** symbol of fruitfulness, usually resembling a fruit basket

"She was pregnant so often that it was a wonder she didn't wear a **calathus** on her head as a symbol of her fruitfulness."

This was the word for a flared, vase-shaped basket of fruit worn on the head, symbolizing fruitfulness in Greek and Egyptian art. The word comes from the Greek *klothein*, meaning "to spin," as in spinning, or weaving, a basket.

calcographer (kalKOGruf*er*) one who draws with crayons

"This child, who was once a talented **calcographer**, is quickly becoming a talented painter."

calf (kaf) an island near a larger one; a small mass of floating ice, separated from a glacier or iceberg

"We needed to navigate away from the **calf** so that the ice wouldn't harm our ship."

calligraphy (kuLIGrufē) beautiful handwriting

"She was impressed by the **calligraphy** on the invitation."

For information about the *calli* root, see "Kallikak."

Cassandra (kuSANdru) a person whose warnings of misfortune are disregarded

"Like Cassandra, the politicians who warned against governmental overspending appear doomed to be ignored."

In classical mythology, Cassandra was a prophetess in Troy during the Trojan War whose predictions, though true, were never believed. Although Apollo gave her the gift of prophecy, he made it worthless when she refused his romantic advances.

Often the term "Cassandra" is used to describe someone who predicts bad news, but it can be used also in the original sense of someone whose accurate prophecies won't be taken seriously.

catadromous (kuTADrumus) swimming downstream, especially to spawn

"The **catadromous** eel departed his freshwater domain and headed out to the open sea."

catagelophobia   (katujelōFŌbēu)   fear of being ridiculed

"The politician's **catagelophobia** caused him not to do or say anything for which he might be criticized later, should he decide to run again for office."

catagraph   (KATugraf)   first draft

"The teacher complained, 'This essay is in no condition to be handed in; what you have here is a **catagraph**, at best.'"

catarolysis   (katuROLisis)   letting off steam by cursing

"The pedantic and money-hungry psychologist explained that the foul-mouthed child's profanity was a serious case of **catarolysis**, which might require extensive observation, testing, and even X-rays to treat fully."

charette, charrette   (shuRET)   a final intensive effort to finish a project before a deadline

"If the **charette** failed, blastoff would once again have to be delayed."

This Old French name for a two-wheeled cart, related to the Old French and English word "chariot," is now applied specifically to the final effort to finish a project in architectural design. This usage may have arisen from the idea that architects' drawings were once hurriedly transported in carts to the construction site.

The *char* in "charette" ultimately comes from the Indo-European *kers*, meaning "to run." From *kers* we now have all these words that are related in meaning: "**car**," "**car**t," "**car**riage," "**car**ry," "**car**eer" (originally, a race course and still sometimes considered a rat race), "**car**penter" (originally from *artifex carpentarius*, "carriage-maker"), "**cour**se," "**cur**riculum" (literally, a running course, or course of study), and "**cor**ridor" (a passageway, especially for running through).

charientism   (KĀRēin•tiz′m)   an insult so gracefully veiled as to seem unintended

  "When the sarcastic gym teacher said that the awkward student's movements were entertaining, we felt that the teacher had delivered a **charientism**."

chiaroscuro   (kyoruSKY*U*ro)   light and shade, black and white

  "Like itself must be perceived as a bit of **chiaroscuro**—nothing entirely black, nothing entirely white."

chiliagon   (KILyugon)   an enclosed figure with one thousand sides

  "The philosopher Descartes held that one can understand what a **chiliagon** is without being able to form a mental image of such a figure."

chimera   (kĭMIRu)   a vain, impossible, or idle fancy

  "Air flight was once considered a **chimera**, worthy only of dreamers."

chirotony (kīROTunē)   an election by a show of hands

"Instead of using secret ballots, we chose our officers in a public way, by conducting a **chirotony**."

This word literally means, quite logically, "stretched" (*ton*) "hand" (*chir*)." The *ton* (or *ten*) root appears in a number of words related to stretching or straining, or to things that are thin or stretched, such as the strings of a musical instrument, and therefore pitch. For example, "**ton**e," "**ton**ic" (medicine that restores or increases body tone), "bari**tone**" (deep tone), "**ten**don," "**ten**se" (tightly stretched), "**ten**uous" (thin strands, hence weak in the sense of having little substance), "con**tend**" (to stretch or strive in order to maintain an assertion or deal with something), "os**ten**tation" (stretching so as to exhibit), "**thin**," "por**tend**" (literally, to stretch out before), "te**tan**us" (disease characterized by muscular contraction; the *ton* root is doubled here), "continue" (stretch out in time—hence, hold out), "**tent**" (stretched canvas), and so on. Note, however, that the word "atone" is *not* related to those words: it is literally from the words "at one." (For information on the *chir* root, see "para**chr**onism.")

circumforaneous (serkum • fuRĀnēus)   wandering from house to house

"The **circumforaneous** man would visit every house long enough to offer to work for food."

First, the *for* in this word and the *fer* in "circumference" are entirely unrelated.

"Circum**for**aneous," which also means "going about from market to market," contains a root, *for*, that is directly related to "**for**um," the name for the ancient Roman marketplace and center of public affairs. In fact, *for* comes ultimately from the Indo-European root *dhwer*, meaning "door"—that is, the entrance to an area surrounding the house—from which we also get the word "door" as well as "**for**est" (the out-of-doors), "**for**eign," "**for**eclose" (shut out, preclude), "**for**ensic" (literally, of the market or forum—hence, public), "**for**feit," "**hor**s d'oeuvre" (literally, outside of work, hence outside the main meal), and possibly "**ur**ban" (out of the countryside).

civil death (SIvul deth) the legal status of one who has been deprived of civil rights

"Under their legal system convicted murderers forfeited all civil rights and suffered **civil death**."

claqueur (klaK*ER*) a member of an audience paid to applaud

"Her goal was to be a **claqueur** in every infomercial."

cleocentric (klēōSENtrik) pertaining to the belief that fame is everything

"The obscure actor was so **cleocentric** that he would do anything for publicity."

cleptobiosis (kleptō · bi*Ō*sis), **lestobiosis** (lestō · bi*Ō*sis) a mode of existence in which one species steals food from another, as certain ants

"The liberal professor dubiously maintained that some poor people resort to stealing food not because of a

44

moral deficiency but rather because of a disease called **cleptobiosis**."

The *clept* in "**clept**obiosis" comes directly from the ancient Indo-European root, *klep* (to steal). This rare root also appears in "**klep**tomania (or "**clep**tomania") and "**clep**sydra," the name of an ancient clock that marked the flow of water, from the Latin *klepsudra* (water stealer).

The *lest* in "**lest**obiosis" comes from the Greek *leistes* (robber). The root ultimately is related to the root of "**lucr**ative" (producing wealth).

cliack   (KLĪuk)   the last armful of grain cut in a harvest

"He was exhausted by the time he grabbed the **cliack**."

clinophobia   (klīnōFŌbēu)   fear of going to bed

"In *Nightmare on Elm Street* those who knew about Freddy were sometimes thought to suffer from **clinophobia**."

conchology   (kongKOLujē)   collecting shells

"Her childhood experiences on the beach introduced her to a lifelong love of **conchology**."

concinnity   (kunSINutē)   harmony and fitness of parts to a whole or to one another

"In the eighteenth century it was common for theologians to refer to the **concinnity** of our body parts in an effort to prove cosmic design."

The *cinn* part of this word comes from the Latin *cinnus*, a mixed drink, the idea of being of something aptly mixed together.

concretize   (KONkrētiz)   to make concrete something abstract

"You need to **concretize** your dreams if you are to succeed in life."

confabulation   (cunFAB • yuLĀshun)   a fabrication of experiences, often to make up for a gap in memory (psychology)

"We weren't sure whether his entire story was accurately recalled or distorted by **confabulation**."

confelicity   (konfiLISitē)   pleasure in others' happiness

"When the nurse told us that she felt happy when she gave others pleasure, she was endorsing the ideal of **confelicity**."

congeries   (KONjurēs)   an aggregation of ideas or things

"The philosopher contemptuously dismissed her colleague's argument as a **congeries** of fallacies."

consensus gentium   (GENtēum)   **fallacy**   the fallacy of arguing that an idea is true because most people believe it or because it has been accepted throughout history

"To argue that some supernatural beings must exist because every generation has believed in them is to commit the **consensus gentium fallacy**."

cowcat (*KOW*kat) a person whose main function is to occupy space

"We need active, thoughtful allies, not simply **cow-cats**."

craquelure (kraKL*U'*r) the web of hairline cracks in the surface of an old painting

"One indication of a painting's age is **craquelure** in its surface."

critouns (KRITunz) frying pan refuse

"He was so hungry that he ate even the **critouns** from the frying pan."

cryptoscopophilia (kriptu • skōpuFILyu) the desire to look into the windows of homes that one passes

"I considered the Peeping Tom they caught a criminal, though a psychiatrist friend told me he was suffering from **cryptoscopophilia**."

cumyxaphily (kyuMIKSufilē) collecting matchboxes

"She would go to bars, restaurants, and hotels just to indulge her passion for **cumyxaphily**."

The *myxa* part of this word comes directly from the Medieval Latin word of the same spelling meaning "lamp wick." From the same word comes ultimately our word "match."

The *myxa* root comes from the Indo-European root,

meug, meaning (slimy, or slippery, hence the slimy, slippery candle wax). That root has given us "**smock**" (protective shirt that usually gets messy), "**muggy**," "**muc**ous," "**moist**," and "**must**y." (See also "**emunction**.")

cunctatious   (kunkTĀshus)   addicted to delaying

"You can forget about finishing on time when you hire **cunctatious** workers."

D

daub   (d*aw*b)   a poorly painted picture

"The art critic insisted that not all paintings are equal and that a Rembrandt painting must be distinguished from a **daub**."

"Daub" comes from the Latin *dealbare*, meaning "to whitewash" or, literally, "to whiten (*albare*) completely (*de*)." *Alb* is a root that appears in a number of English words relating to whiteness, including "**al-bino**," "**albumen**," and "**aub**ade" (song sung when lovers part at daybreak—when the bright, shiny sun rises). (For more about "white" words, see "**alb**escent.")

deaconing   (DĒKuning)   the practice of packing food so that the finest specimens are visible

"They are engaged in ideological **deaconing** in which they hide their less attractive ideas under their most attractive ones to appeal to unwary and gullible individuals."

deadset   (DEDset)   a hunting dog's stance

"He stood as if in a **deadset**, about to pounce upon his prey."

debridement (diBRĒDmawn)   the surgical removal of dead or contaminated tissue from a wound to prevent infection

"Many Nazis believed in a kind of cultural **debridement** in which hated people would be removed from the society of good, 'healthy' people."

deciduous (diSIJuwus)   falling off or shedding, as petals, leaves, and fruit

"I wanted both evergreen and **deciduous** trees."

decubitus (diKYUbitus)   the position a patient assumes in bed

"They were surprised to see you **decubitus**, since you are nearly always on your feet engaged in some vital activities."

The *cubitus* part of this word relates directly to lying down. The word comes from the Latin *decumbere* (to lie down). In fact, the *cumbere* part of "decumbere" means, by itself, "to lie down." The *de-* prefix, which means "down," apparently serves only to emphasize that one in such a position is lying down *very much*. In other words, one is lying down out of necessity, not for mere relaxation, and probably for a longer period than usual—hence suggesting illness.

defenestrate (dēFENu • strāt)   to throw out of a window

"The burglar was caught **defenestrating** my stereo speakers."

defenestration (dēfenuSTRĀshun)   the act of throwing something or someone out of a window

"People used to throw sewage and trash out of their windows but today such **defenestration** is illegal."

denouement (dānuMAWN)   the unraveling of a dramatic literary plot

"This tense matter has finally reached its **denouement**, so that we now learn how the conflict was resolved."

dereism (DĒrēiz'm)   the tendency to regard life through daydreams and fantasies, with little regard to reality

"He can distinguish between dreams and reality and shows no sign of **dereism**."

despumate (DESpyumāt)   to remove impurities from the skin

"She regards criminals as scum and holds that such people must be **despumated** if the streets are to be safe."

desterilize (dēSTERiliz)   to use money or a commodity previously unused

"They were delighted when gold was **desterilized** as backing for credit and new currency."

deus ex machina   (DĀus • eksMAKunu)   one who unexpectedly intervenes to change the course of events

> "To Clinton, Ross Perot was a **deus ex machina**,
> siphoning off votes that would have gone to President
> Bush."

The phrase is Latin for "a god from a machine." It
denotes the practice of some Greek playwrights, such as
Euripides, to end the drama with a god who, after being
lowered to the stage by a mechanical apparatus, would solve
the problems of the human characters.

Today the phrase is often used for any forced and
improbable device, such as an unexpected inheritance, by
which an author resolves the plot. Charles Dickens's *Oliver
Twist* contains a deus ex machina, as does Thomas Hardy's
Tess of the D'Urbervilles.

deuterogamist   (d*uter*OGumist)   a widow or widower
who remarries

> "In the television show 'The Brady Bunch,' both
> parents were presumably **deuterogamists**, since script-
> writers didn't want to present them as divorced."

dextrovert   (DEKstru • ve*r*t)   turning to the right

> "This country began to **dextrovert** under Ronald
> Reagan."

discalceate   (diSKALsēit)   to take one's shoes off

> "In some cultures you are expected to **discalceate** as
> you enter people's homes."

discophily (diSKOFilē) collecting phonograph records

"Since the advent of CDs, fewer people have engaged in **discophily**."

disembosom (disimBUZum) to release from an embrace; to get something off one's chest

"It was years before she felt she could **disembosom** her secret."

The major part of this word is "bosom" (chest). The *bo* part of "**bo**som" comes from the Indo-European root *beu* (swelling). The *beu* root ultimately contributed to such English words as "**po**cket" (*b* became *p* in Germanic languages), "**po**ut" (blow out the cheeks), "**bu**cket," "**bo**il," "**bo**ast," "**bub**ble," "**bo**wl" (in the sense of a bowling ball), "e**bu**llient," "**bu**ccal" (pertaining to the cheek), "**bu**ckle," from the Latin *buccula* (literally little cheek, but originally the cheek strap of a helmet), and so on.

disgorger (disGAWRj*er*) instrument used to remove a hook from the mouth of a fish

"We might need a **disgorger** to remove his foot from his mouth."

dishabille (DISubēl) partly or carelessly dressed

"The men wanted to see the actress in **dishabille**."

dishabillophobia (DISu • BĒLu • FŌbēu) fear of undressing in front of someone

"Because her modesty bordered on **dishabillophobia**, she insisted on undressing apart from all the other nurses."

doppelgänger (DOPulGANG*er*) ghostly double of someone not yet dead

"The twins would haunt each other like **doppelgängers**."

doyen (D*OI*[y]en) the senior member of a group, society, or profession

"The founding partner was the **doyen** of the law firm."

dub, palooka (dub, puLUKu) an incompetent, easily defeated athlete, especially a boxer.

"George Foreman almost decapitated the **palooka**, who was clearly out of his depth."

The origin of "dub" in this sense relates probably to the idea of being a poor hitter. One who was dubbed a knight was literally tapped (hit lightly) on the shoulder with a sword. In golf, dubbing is hitting the ball poorly. Ultimately, "dub" comes from the same word as "dowel," which is basically a kind of stick. And a stick, of course, can be used for hitting. Remember, too, that the letters *b*, *v*, and *w* are linguistically related; thus, "dub" is related to the sound *duv*, which is related to the sound *duw* or *dow* or, in this case, "dowel."

Note, however, that the "dub" here has nothing to do with dubbing, say, a musical recording. That kind of "dub" is simply short for "double," since the recording is literally being doubled, or duplicated.

"Palooka" may derive from the awkward boxing champion, Joe Palooka, the hero of a comic strip drawn by Ham Fisher.

dun (1) to make repeated and insistent demands upon, especially for the payment of a debt; (2) a person who duns another; (3) an insistent demand for payment

"The collections department **dunned** him for his bills."

dysanagnosia (disANagNŌzyu) the inability to understand some words

"Even though he suffered from **dysanagnosia**, he could understand most commonly used words."

dyscalligynia (dis • kaliJINēu) dislike of beautiful women

"The large woman, who was trying in vain to lose weight, evinced intense **dyscalligynia** whenever a slim woman walked by."

dysnomy (DISnumē) bad legislation; the passage of bad laws

"When I accused the legislator of sponsoring **dysnomy**, he smiled and said, 'That's how I get reelected.' "

E

eidetic (īDETik) of or pertaining to complete visual memory

"People with excellent photographic memories are known for their lifelike **eidetic** imagery."

eidolism (Īdu • liz′m) belief in ghosts

"Although many scientists are skeptical about the existence of ghosts, **eidolism** is fairly common among members of the public."

eidolon (īDŌlun) an ideal person or thing

"Contrary to the impressions their publicists try to promote, neither Michael Jordan nor Michael Jackson is an **eidolon**.

eisegesis (ĪSuJĒsis) a biased interpretation, especially of Scripture

"Each biblical scholar accused the other of resorting to **eisegesis** rather than looking at the Bible without bias."

elapidation (ēlapuDĀshun)   a clearing away of stones

"Fred Flintstone's job involved **elapidation** in a quarry pit."

empleomania (emplēōMĀnēu)   an uncontrollable passion for holding public office

"Our senior senator, who has run for over fifteen offices, suffers from severe **empleomania**."

emulous (EMyulus)   wishing to equal

"That **emulous** woman has great intelligence and will most likely surpass her male rivals in her department."

emunction (ēMUNKshun)   the act or process of picking or blowing the nose

"When she pulled out the tissue, placed it next to her nose, and engaged in **emunction** at the dinner table, the other guests gave her dirty looks."

The key to the meaning of this word is in the *mu* part. A number of words that begin with *mu*, *my*, or *mo* relate to dampness, flowing, or sliminess and have similar linguistic origins. For example, "**mu**cus," "**mo**ist," "**mu**d," "**mu**ggy," "**my**riad" (in the sense of flowing to the point of uncountability), "**mu**sty," "**mo**ss," which is found in swamps. Further, *myc* or *myco* is a prefix for words denoting types of fungi, and *myx* or *myxo*, for types of slime. Even the *mu* in the word "s**mu**ggle" is related to the idea of sliminess—in the sense of slipping through. Further, a s**m**ock is a garment you can slip on over your clothes.

Note that "emunctory" is a term for any part of the body that carries off waste matter, such as skin or kidneys. (See also "**cumyx**aphily.")

enatation   (ēnāTĀshun)   escaping by swimming

"Our navy seals must be skillful at **enatation**."

encopresis   (enkuPRĒsis)   unintentional defecation [also, perhaps a nice alternative to the phrase, "s——ing in one's pants"]

"If he knew that his entire fortune was gone, he would have to clean his pants from **encopresis**."

endogamy   (enDOGumē)   marriage within one's group or tribe

"The Orthodox Jew encourages his family to practice **endogamy**, since he believes that mixed marriages are a threat to the preservation of the faith."

enew   (eNY*U*)   to plunge someone or something into water

"People who are intensely afraid of water shouldn't be **enewed**."

The *en* part of this word means simply "in." The *ew* means "water" and ultimately originates from Indo-European *akwa*—*aqua*, that is. The French version, *eau* or *ewe*, has led to not only "en**ew**" but also to "s**ew**er" (ultimately from *exaqua*) and "**ea**ger" (literally, water-spear—a tidal wave).

epitrope (ePITrupē) conceding a point in an argument in such a way as to belittle the point or ridicule the opponent or the opponent's position

> "When the woman conceded to the conservative that the government clearly overregulates our lives, we knew that her concession was an **epitrope**, on the basis of which she would later argue against the conservative's defense of drug laws."

equalitarian (ēkwoluTERēun) pertaining to the doctrine that all people are equal

> "As a libertarian, she cannot accept an **equalitarian** view that endorses the redistribution of wealth so that all people get equal portions, regardless of their actions."

equilibrist (ēkwuLIBrist), **schoenabatist** (skēNABut-ist) a tightrope walker

> "**Equilibrists** often attract larger audiences when there are no safety nets under the tightrope."

equiponderate (ēkwuPONdurāt) to make equal in importance or weight

> "To **equiponderate** my friend and me, my uncle gave me a thirty-pound dumbbell to use while seesawing with my heavier friend."

The *pond* in this word ultimately comes from the Indo-European root, *(s)pend* (stretch, spin, hang, and hence weight or weigh on the mind). The root has given us "pound," "preponderance" (a greater weight), "ponder," "suspend," "suspense," "pendant" (it hangs), "pensive" (weighing, pondering, thinking), "spin," "spider" (spins a web—from the Germanic *spithra*), "span," "append" (literally, to weigh, hence to add to), "depend" (hang from, hence rely on), "compendium" (a weighing together, hence an overview or summary of a larger work), "penthouse" (an appendage of a house), "stipend" (literally, a weighed gift, hence payment for services), "propensity" (hanging before, hence leaning toward a particular area or direction), "compensate" (to weigh, hence to make equal or to offset), "recompense," "spend" (to weigh out, hence to pay out), "expend," and "poise" (ultimately from Latin *pensare*, to ponder—that is, to weigh, hence to maintain balance).

erotetic (eruTETik), **pysmatic** (pizMATik) pertaining to asking quetions

> "Instead of making statements, Socrates preferred **erotetic** discourse."

erotodromomania (ēROtu·DROmu·MĀnyu) pathological desire to travel so as to escape from an upsetting sexual experience

> "We weren't sure whether she liked to travel or whether her travel was a form of **erotodromomania** to forget her many unpleasant sexual relationships."

erotomania (irotuMĀnēu) obsession with sex

> "Because of their obsession with X-rated videos, and obscene rock lyrics, Americans have been accused of **erotomania**."

ersatz (*ER*zots) a substitute, often of inferior quality

"Sea Legs, though tolerable, are at best **ersatz** crab-meat."

ethos (Ḗth*aws*) character and attitudes of a community or an individual

"Those straitlaced, hardworking, and extremely religious people felt uncomfortable in the **ethos** of the French Quarter of New Orleans."

etui, etwee (Ā́twē) a case for small articles such as needles

"We were surprised to see the large, rough man carrying the needles in an **etui**."

"Etui" comes from the Old French *estui* (prison). Ultimately, it comes from Vulgar Latin *estudiare* (to treat carefully), the connection being that guarding a person requires careful overseeing. The ultimate origin is the Latin *studium* (study) and is the source of the word "study."

The plural, "etuis" (pronounced āTWĒZ), gave us "tweezer," one of the instruments typically contained in an etui.

eudaemonia (y*u*dēMŌNēu) happiness or well-being resulting from a life of virtue and moderation

"Aristotle believed that people could attain **eudaemonia** if they had good moral habits and some degree of luck."

euhemerism (y*u*HĒmuriz′m) the theory that all myths are based on reality, especially that they're exaggerations of true stories about real people

"The scholar, devoted to **euhemerism**, believed that many of the pagan gods weren't entirely imaginary but were exaggerations of certain national figures."

exemplar (egZEMPl*er*)   one who is regarded as worthy of imitation

"We need more **exemplars** and fewer bad role models."

The *em* part of this word is an Indo-European root that originally meant "take" and then "buy" (a form of taking). It has given us a number of other English words, including "rede**em**" (to buy back or take back), "pr**em**ium" (an award, an inducement to buy, an unusual value), "pro**m**pt" (to bring forth, to make manifest), "pres**um**e," "ass**um**e" (take, as in to take responsibility and to take for granted), "s**um**ptuous" (of something so splendid that it must have been bought for a high price), "pre**em**pt" (to take before others take), "s**am**ple" (to take a little), and "rans**om**" (a type of buying), as well as "ex**am**ple" (something taken out as representative or illustrative), and "ex**em**plify."

exoculate (eksOKy*u*lāt)   to put out the eyes of

"Movies that explicitly show people copulating will receive an X-rating, but those that explicitly show someone **exoculating** a victim will recive an R-rating or possibly even an R-17 rating if the movie is sufficiently artsy."

exogamy (ekSOGum̄ē)   marriage outside one's group or tribe

"Parents who want their children to marry within their religion or ethnic group may not necessarily be bigoted. They may simply believe that **exogamy** threatens the continuation of their heritage and tradition."

exordium   (egZORdēum)   the opening part of a speech

"An effective **exordium** will usually grab the attention of the listeners and make them feel that the speaker is friendly."

expeditio   (eks•puDISHēō)   quickly dismissing minor points to come to the main point

"I thought she was going to dismiss my entire argument until I discovered that she was engaging in **expeditio**."

F

fagin (FĀgin) a teacher of crime

"In prison a young person can find a **fagin** who will teach him to refine his criminal skills."

fallacy (FALusē) **of the beard** the fallacy of using an oversimple quantifiable part of a problem, as in the argument that doing this just one more day won't make any difference; the fallacy that occurs when someone denies the legitimacy of a distinction by pointing out vague cases to which the distinction cannot apply with mathematical precision, as when someone suggests that the distinction between day and night is of dubious value because there are times when one can't say when one day ends and the other begins

"When she claimed that, because there is no sharp distinction between middle age and old age, the distinction is without any basis, we knew she was committing the **fallacy of the beard**."

fard (fawrd) to put on makeup

"She pulled out her cosmetics and began **farding**."

fastigium (fasTIJēum)   the most critical and serious moment of an illness

"We were lucky she was in the hospital during the **fastigium**."

fenestella (fenuSTELu), **wicket**   a small window

"In a Roman Catholic church it is common for a **fenestella** to be in the south wall of the sanctuary near the altar."

fenestral (fiNEStrul)   pertaining to windows

"The glassmaker is well informed about virtually all matters **fenestral**."

fenestrated (FINustrātud)   having windows

"Instead of saying that we needed more windows, our English teacher told us that she wanted our school to be more highly fenestrated."

In Latin, *fenestra* meant "an opening in the wall"—that is, a window. The origin of the Latin word is obscure.

festination (festiNĀshun)   the act of walking faster and faster, as when going down a long, steep slope

"His walking was slow but then speeded up, especially downhill, when he achieved maximal **festination**."

"Festination" comes from the Latin *festinare* (to make haste). It is embodied in the saying of the Roman historian

Suetonius (second century A.D.), "*Festina lente*" (Make haste slowly). Some writers speculate that *festina* and "haste" both originate from the same Germanic root, *haifsti*.

firebreak (FYer•brāk) a strip of land that has been plowed or cleared to prevent the spread of fire

"Because the farmers had plowed a **firebreak** around their land, the fire was contained."

flanerie (FLANrē) idle walking

"Are you going somewhere or just enjoying **flanerie**?"

fleabite (flē•bīt) minor pain

"It isn't an intense pain, only a **fleabite**."

Fletcherize (FLE*cher*īz) to chew throughly, specifically, thirty times for each mouthful

"I was instructed to eat more slowly and **Fletcherize** my food."

flotsam (FLOTsum) wreckage that is afloat or washed up on the shore

"Those sleeping around skid row were considered **flotsam**, drifting without connection to other human beings."

fnast (fnast), **fnese** (fnēz) to breathe hard

"Running up many flights of stairs caused him to **fnast**."

foma (FŌmu)   harmless untruths

"My parents told me that the belief in Santa Claus is a **foma**."

fomites (FAWmutēz)   any agents, as clothing or bedding, capable of absorbing and transmitting infectious organisms

"The dirty, bacteria-infected dishes were almost certainly the **fomites** through which his disease was transmitted."

footcandle (fut • kand'l)   an amount of light thrown by a candle (on one square foot of surface one foot away)

"The UFO instantly sprayed the area with a brilliant light that must have been thousands of **footcandles**."

forfoughten (f*er*FOC*H*ten)   exhausted from fighting

"The boxer was so **forfoughten** after the fight that he could hardly walk or even talk."

The *fought* part of this word is, of course, related to "fight." It descends from Old English *fohten* and, ultimately, the Indo-European *pek* (to comb or to pluck). By extension, *pek* means also "fight" (which might, after all, involve plucking hair), "woolly animals" (which can be plucked), and "money" (since cattle and sheep can be sold). From that root we now have "**pec**toral" (of the chest, which, in males, is often hairy), "**pec**uliar" (one's own, from Latin *peculium*: wealth in cattle), "**pec**uniary" (pertaining to or requiring money), "**fee**" (*p* and *f* are closely related), "**feu**dal," and "fellow" (from Old Norse **felagi**: one who lays down money, as in a joint undertaking, hence partner).

formication (formiKĀshun) the feeling that ants or other bugs are crawling on one

"The man began to spray his body with insecticide because of his **formication**."

formicide (*FOR*Mucīd) killing of ants; a substance used to kill ants

"I'm not a violent person, but I must confess that when the ants overran our picnic I had **formicide** on my mind."

The main roots of the word are *formic* (ant), and *cide* (kill).

G

galericulate (gal*er*IKy*u*let)   covered with a hat

"Although today most American men go around hat-
less, men in the 1950s were usually **galericulate**."

gallinicide (guLINisīd)   the killing of chickens or turkeys

"She was a vegetarian except during Thanksgiving,
when she considered **gallinicide** only a venial sin."

That the *gall* in "gallinicide" looks and sounds like "call"
is no coincidence. For chickens and turkeys do a lot of
calling. The ancient roots *gal* and *gar* (cry, shout, call) were
formed from the sound of a cry, shout, or call. From those
roots we have "**care**" which originally meant "to lament" or
"to cry, "**garrulous**" (chattering, talkative), and "**Ger**man,"
the Celtic name for the Germanii who came (loudly) into
battle. Finally, "slogan" comes from the Gaelic *sluagh-
ghairm* (war cry). Indeed, a slogan is the war cry of
bureaucrats.

gam (gam)   a visit at sea or ashore, as a friendly conversation between whalers

"The sailors enjoyed a **gam** in which they related their experiences at sea."

gambler's fallacy (GAMblerz FALusē)   an argument that something will occur because it hasn't yet occurred

"To think that a coin that has come up heads ten times in a row must turn up tails on the eleventh flip is to commit the **gambler's fallacy**."

gambrinous (gamBRĪnus)   full of beer

"After receiving the beer bong, the fraternity boy rubbed his bloated, **gambrinous** gut."

gapeseed (GĀPsēd)   a sight or event that draws a crowd of idle spectators

"The fire was the **gapeseed** attracting rubberneckers."

gerascophobia (jerASkō • FŌbēu)   fear of growing old

"He dyed his gray hair black, had a facelift, constantly used hip talk, and, in short, showed all the signs of **gerascophobia**."

geratology (jiriTOLugē)   study of the breaking down or aging of things

"The wisecracking used-car salesman claimed that his 'extensive knowledge of **geratology**' allowed him to offer the opinion that this used car would last many more years before it breaks down."

gerontocracy (jerunTOKrusē) government by old people

"Although it certainly was not a democracy, the former Soviet Union, which rarely had top leaders under sixty years old, was a true **gerontocracy**."

girouettism (SZHIRwutiz′m) the practice of frequently altering one's opinions to follow popular trends

"Politicians often become so expert at **girouettism** that no one knows what they really believe."

gixlety (GIKs′ltē) the overuse of kind words or actions

"Measured praise is enjoyed, but **gixlety** is usually regarded with suspicion."

gongoozler (gonGUZler) one who spends an inordinate amount of time staring at things that are out of the ordinary

"The crowd of **gongoozlers** wouldn't stop staring at the accident until the paramedics took the injured people away."

gorget (GORjit) throat armor

"Knights at times needed a **gorget** to protect against throat wounds."

gowpen (GU • u • pen) hands cupped to form a bowl

"He formed his hands into a **gowpen** as he drank from the lake."

71

gowyop (*GOW*yup) a state of perplexity in which familiar persons or things seem strange, as when someone you have not seen for years looks so different that you cannot place him

"My mind had fallen into a **gowyop**, in which my old school looked quite alien to me."

grandgosier (gron • *guz*YO) one who will swallow anything

"Anything you put in front of him, the **grandgosier** will eat."

grangerize (GRĀNj*er*īz) to tear illustrations out of a book

"Since the elderly man was obsessed with pictures of young women, he would **grangerize** picture-books to make his own collection."

gravamen (gruVĀmun) the part of an accusation that weighs most heavily or importantly against the accused; the most significant or telling part of a grievance

"We asked them to forget insignificant complaints and give us only their **gravamen**."

gressorial (greSŌrēul) adapted for walking

"Our legs are **gressorial**, as any walker will tell you."

"Gressorial" originates from Latin *gradus, gressum* (walk). Other descendants of those words include "**grad**e" and words ending in -*grade* and -*gradient*, "**grad**ual," "**grad**uation," "de**grade**" (step down, hence reduce, lower), "in**gress**" (step in, enter), "in**gred**ient" (literally, enter, as a constituent that enters into the mixture), "ag**gress**ion" (a going to, an attack), "trans**gress**ion" (a stepping across), and "con**gress**" (a going or coming together).

H

hadeharia   (hādēHORēu)   constant use of the word "hell"

"Our preacher, who is known for his **hadeharia**, uses the language of hell much more often than that of heaven."

hagiarchy   (HAGē*awr*kē)   government by persons considered holy

"John Calvin tried to establish a **hagiarchy** in Geneva."

hallux   (HALuks)   the big toe

"While her little toes were cute, her **hallux** was beautiful, at least to her boyfriend, a foot fetishist."

halobios   (halōBĪus)   sea flora and fauna

"He loved deep sea diving because it gave him a personal view of the **halobios**."

The sea is that large body of salt water that covers much of this planet. And "salt" is the significant word here. "Salt" and several other English words descend from *sal*, the Latin word for "salt." They include "salami" (a heavily salted food), "sauce," "sausage," "salad," and "salary" (originally the payment of salt to soldiers, used to preserve their food when on the march).

In the sense that saltiness is strong to the taste, peppy (as is also pepper, for example), and lively, the *sal* root has also given us words that, at least in their origins, pertain to liveliness and good health. For example, "lusty" (from Latin *salus*), "salute" (to wish good health to), "salutary" (beneficial, conducive to good health), "salvage" (preserved, saved from harm), "save," "salvation," "salubrious" (conducive to good health, wholesome), and "sylvan" (pertaining to the forest, which is a salubrious place). See also "xylophilous."

The Greek word for "salt sea"—*hals* (the Greek *h*, and *sh*, being closely related to the Latin *s*)—has given us words with the *halo-* prefix, including "halobios" (literally, sea life).

hamartia (ham*awr*TĒu) the single defect of character in an otherwise decent person, sometimes referred to as the tragic flaw

"Some commentators held that Senator Gary Hart's **hamartia** was his desire for punishment, which was satisfied by getting caught in what appeared to be an adulterous relationship."

hamartophobia (haM*AW*RtōFŌbēu) fear of sin or sinning

"The liberal church historian believed that Saint Paul's concern with sin bordered on **hamartophobia**."

heliotropic (hēlēuTROPik)   growing toward the sun or light

"When we exposed the plant to sunlight, we quickly discovered that it was **heliotropic**."

hemianopsia (hemē・uNOPsēu)   half or partial blindness

"When it comes to reading these somewhat biased reports I use a sort of **hemianopsia**, ignoring the rhetoric and studying only the claims that are supported with evidence."

henotheism (HĒnōthēiz'm)   belief in one god while not necessarily concluding that that is the only god

"The scholar maintained that ancient tribes adhered to **henotheism**, which allowed their special allegiance to certain gods while allowing for the existence of other tribal gods."

heredipety (heruDIPutē)   seeking an inheritance

"The murder was motivated by the **heredipety** of a greedy heir."

The *her* part of this word comes from the Indo-European root, *ghe*, meaning "to lack" or "to go without" (*gh*, *g*, and *h* are related). From that root, we have "heir" (one who gets what's left), "**her**itage," "**her**edity," and other related words.
The origin of the *dipety* ending was influenced by the word "serendipity," which is included in this dictionary.

hereism (HIRēiz′m) fidelity in marriage

"The pastor exhorted us to be true to our marital vows so that we would be known for our **hereism**, not our apistia—infidelity in marriage, that is."

hermeneutics (he*r*muN[Y]*U*tiks) interpretation of literary texts, especially the Bible

"The biblical scholar explained to us that the Bible is not self-interpreting but requires **hermeneutics**, in which systematic scholarship must be applied."

hesternopathia (heSTERnō • PATHēu) a pathological yearning for the good old days

"We need to enjoy today instead of indulging in **hesternopathia**."

The *hester* part of this word comes from the original Indo-European root, *gzehei*, or *ghdhies*, meaning "**yesterday**," which is itself another descendant of that root.

heterogamosis (HEDurō • guMōsis) marriage between persons distinctly unsuitable for each other

"You need to marry a like-minded person, or else you'll be a victim of **heterogamosis** and then possibly divorce."

hieromachy (hī*er*OMukē) a fight between persons of the cloth

"The old cleric said that he was tired of heresies, schisms, and **hieromachy** and wanted to focus on fundamental points of agreement."

hindermate (HINd*er* • māt)   a mate who is a hindrance

"When it came to her career, her jealous husband was a **hindermate**."

hippodamist (hiPODumist)   a city planner

"We need more than one **hippodamist** if we want this new city to fulfill the needs of its inhabitants."

hippomaniac (hipuMĀnēak)   a horse lover

"The equestrian owned several horses and described herself as a **hippomaniac**."

hippopotomonstrosesquipedalian (HIpō • potuMONstrō • seskwupuDĀLēun)   pertaining to a very long word

"When William F. Buckley used the word 'epiphenomenalism,' we knew that he enjoyed using **hippopoto-monstrosesquipedalian** words."

Since this word is itself very long, it can be called an autological (*aw*tuLOjuk'l) word—that is, a word that is an example of what it denotes. In contrast, a word such as "monosyllabic" (having only one syllable) is a heterological (HED*eru*LOjuk'l) word, because it is *not* an example of what it denotes.

hirci (H*ER*sē)   armpit hair

"In parts of Europe women with **hirci** are considered sexy, whereas most American men prefer women to have clean-shaven armpits."

hodophobia (hōdōFŌbēu)   fear of road travel

"When I asked whether she wanted to ride with us to
Charlottesville, she said that her **hodophobia** would
make her uncomfortable during a three-hour ride."

holagogue (HOLug*aw*g)   a medicine that removes all
traces of a disease

"I don't want a pill to get rid of only a few symptoms
of the illness; I want a **holagogue**."

holmgang (HŌLMgang)   a duel fought on an island

"When the two were on the island, each challenged the
other to a **holmgang** to defend the honor of the woman
they loved."

The *gang* part of this word—descended from a root
meaning "going"—is identical with the word with which
we're all too familiar today. A gang is a group of people
literally **going** together, often to "gang up" on some other
group.

The *holm* part of "holmgang" comes from the Indo-
European root, *kel*, meaning "that which is elevated," as a
hill. From it have arisen "**col**umn," "**col**ophon" (publisher's
emblem—literally, a summit, a finishing touch), "**cul**mi-
nate" (to reach the highest point), "ex**cel**" (to raise up, to
elevate), "**col**on," "**col**onel" (originally the leader of a
column of soldiers). In Germanic, the Indo-European *k*
became *h*, led also to "**hil**l" and "**hol**m" (an island in a lake
or river), which also appears in place-names—for example,
Stoc**khol**m.

horripilation (h*o*ripuLĀshun)   goose pimples

"The horror movie took only fifteen minutes to cause **horripilation** in the viewers."

hwyl (HU*i*l)   an eloquent emotional outburst

"His passionate commitment to his cause prompted him to respond with a **hwyl** that people quote even today."

hygeiolatry (hījēOLutrē)   fanaticism about one's health

"It's one thing to be prudent about one's health, quite another to fall victim to **hygeiolatry**."

hypengyophobia (hīPENjēō • FŌbēu)   fear of responsibility

"The eminent dissenting psychiatrist held that many people who choose to act like children and to reject personal responsibility have **hypengyophobia**."

hyperurbanism (hip*erER*b'niz'm)   overcorrect usage or exaggerated pronunciation that results from trying to avoid provincial-sounding English, as in the improper use of "I" instead of "me" in "between you and I" or in the pronunciation of the *t* in "often"

"Since he was upwardly mobile and was unsure about pronunciations, he would sometimes overreach and fall victim to **hyperurbanism**."

hypnopedia (hipnuPĒdēu)   the process of learning while asleep—by listening to a recording, for example

"Although I've heard that the Russians have experimented with **hypnopedia**, I believe that learning is possible only when people are awake."

hypobulia   (hīpōBYU̅lēu)   difficulty in making decisions

"The president seems to have **hypobulia**, since he is indecisive about virtually every major issue that confronts him."

I

iatrapistia (īatruPIStēu)   lack of faith in doctors or medicine

> "When the Christian Scientist said she believed that illnesses represent spiritual difficulties and that people need prayer far more than they need medical doctors, the physician accused her of **iatrapistia**."

The original root of the *iatra* part of this word is the same as the root of such words as "**ir**ate" and "**ir**e." The original root of all those words, *eis*, meant "to set in rapid motion." One can see how the act of setting into rapid motion would relate to wrath and anger, hence "irate."

The *eis* root also meant "great power," the connection between setting in motion and having great power being most likely that people with power can set things in rapid motion. And what does power have to do with doctors? Need you ask?

Actually, doctors have—or so we believe—the power to heal. The Greek word for healer was *iatros*, which originated from the Greek word for holy, *hieros*, which in turn comes from the *eis* root. The *iatr* root appears not only in words beginning with *iatra* and *iatro*, but also in such words as "ped**iatr**ician," "ger**iatr**ics," and "pod**iatr**y."

iatrogenic (īatrōJENik) diseases or symptoms that are caused by doctors

"When the physician accidentally infected his patient, his patient's illness was labeled **iatrogenic**."

iatromisia (īatrōMĒzēu) dislike of doctors

"I don't have **iatromisia**; I just think that I can take care of myself better than doctors can."

iatrophobia (īatrōFŌbēu) fear of going to the doctor

"Before his **iatrophobia** was cured, he couldn't get within a city block of a doctor."

iconoclast (īKONuklast) one who attacks or ridicules cherished beliefs, ideals, and customs

"Every age requires **iconoclasts** if people are to continue to grow and adapt to changes."

iconolagny (ī·kuNOL′gnē) sexual stimulation by means of pictures

"I buy *Playboy* not because of **iconolagny** but rather for its articles."

ictal (IKtul) **emotions** suddenly occurring and vanishing emotions, especially depression and anxiety

"We were told that some, but not all, forms of depression are **ictal emotions**, simply short-lived responses to unpleasant events."

illachrymable   (iLAKrimub′l)   unable to cry

"Unfeeling and **illachrymable**, my sociopathic neighbor couldn't generate enough sentiment to produce even one tear over my tax audit."

The *lachrym* part of this word comes from the Latin word *lacrima*, which is related to the Old Latin *dakruma*. *Dakruma* is, in turn, related to the Gothic word *tagr*, from which—you guessed it—we get "tear." It takes tears, of course, to cry.

Note that the meanings of such words as "illachrymable" and "lacrimation" (weeping) can be more easily remembered by noticing the "cry" in the middle (illa**chry**mable, la**cri**mation). The word "cry" itself, however, is *not* related in origin to either of those words. "Cry" comes from the Latin *quiritare* (to cry out for help from a citizen). A *quiris* was a Roman citizen.

illeism   (ILēiz′m)   reference to oneself in the third person

"We could see right through his **illeism**, for it was clear that the 'he' and 'him' to whom he contantly referred was in fact himself."

imago   (iMĀgō)   an adult insect; an idealized mental image of someone, which remains unaltered long after its formation in infancy

"Her imago of her father hardly reflects the man's abusiveness and insensitivity."

immachination   (imakuNĀshun)   the process of becoming part of a plan or machine

"The **immachination** of every citizen was the mayor's dream, so that everyone could play a part in the city's renewal."

immerd (iM*ERD*) to cover with dung

"The Bible contains a passage in which God threatens to **immerd** lying prophets."

inosculate (inOSky*u*lāt) to join so as to become continuous

"Her novel, set in the past but relevant to today's geopolitical events, is an attempt to **inosculate** present and past."

The word "osculate" means "to kiss," the connection with "inosculate" being that a kiss is a meeting or joining. "Osculate" is laterally "small" (*cul*) "mouth (*os*)."

insilium (inSILyum) legal term for evil advice or counsel

"His advising her to kill is a clear case of **insilium**."

insolate (INsōlāt) to expose to sunlight

"If you want your plants to grow, you'll need to **insolate** them, because without sunlight they'll die."

instant, extra, quickie a book rushed into print, usually to cash in on the public's interest in a recent event or phenomenon

"His rushed biography of Ross Perot is a good example of an **instant**, which wouldn't have been written or published had Perot not run for president."

instar (INSt*er*)   insect form between molts

"This particular **instar** is an insect form known to have seven molts."

instar (inST*A*WR)   to make something or someone a star

"Her Oscar-winning performance **instarred** her."

instauration (INstu • R*A*shun)   restoration to former excellence

"The company's **instauration** will begin with a thorough reappraisal of all current executives and managers."

The *sta* in this word and the *sto* in "restore" have a common, and very popular, root. Indeed, quite a number of words come from the Indo-European root, *sta*, meaning, "to stand" or "to stay," and "things that stand or are strong, firm, solid, hard." These words include "stand," "stet" (Latin: let it stand), "status" (one's standing), "tank" (from Portuguese *tanque*, an accidental shortening of *estanque*: to stop a flow, to dam, to cause to stand), "stance," "circumstance," "substance," "substitute," "institute," "constant," "extant," "distant," "stanza," "instant," "standard," "static" (not moving), "statistics" (which show how things stand, the current state of affairs), "local" (from Old Latin, *stlocus*: a place, a set location), "stable," "install," "stalwart," "stall," "stallion" (a horse kept in a stall), "statue," "sta-

86

tioner" (who sells stationery in a standing—permanent, that is—store), "grand**stand**" (permanent standing bleachers), "**sta**tionary," "e**sta**blish," "home**stead**," "in**stead**" (stand in for), "de**sti**ny" (how things will stand), "con**sti**tution," "ob**sti**nate," "arre**st**" (from Latin *arrestare*: to stand back), "assi**st**," "consi**st**," "resi**st**," "subsi**st**," "**star**" (a standing, or fixed, body in the sky), "**st**ore," "re**st**ore" (to stand again), "re**st**aurant" (for food, which restores us), and on and on.

See also "in**star**" and "**st**ull."

isochrous (īSOKr*uu*s) of uniform color

"Most people are **isochrous**, but certain skin diseases can produce patches of skin whose color differs from that of the rest of the skin."

isocracy (īSOKrusē) government in which all have equal power

"They condemned the ideal of a pure **isocracy** as unrealistic and impracticable, since they held that children and ex-convicts shouldn't have as much power as others, and that political representatives would unavoidably be more powerful than ordinary citizens."

isonomy (īSONumē) equality before the law and in political rights

"They asked not for special privileges or rights, only for **isonomy**."

J

J'adoubovitz (szhoDUBōvits) in chess, a player who annoys his opponent by making constant small adjustments to the pieces

"The fidgety **J'adoubovitz** was so annoying that I couldn't concentrate on the chess game."

The expression comes from *j'adoube*, which is French for "I adjust." The French expression is used by chess players to let their opponents know that they intend to touch a chess piece merely to adjust its position. Custom requires that players say "j'adoube" before touching the pieces. Some players, however, adjust their pieces so frequently that they annoy their opponents, and such people are J'adoubovitzes.

jarovize (YOruvīz) to hasten the development of something—for example, seeds—by some process

"Just as we **jarovize** the flowering plants by exposing partially sprouted seeds to low or high temperatures, we need to **jarovize** our young people's minds by stressing the seeds of intellectual curiosity."

jumboism (JUMbōiz′m) the admiration of things simply because of their largeness

"If it weren't for the high price of gas, I'd find it harder to sell small cars to Americans, whose tastes usually go in the direction of **jumboism**."

juvenescent (j*u*vuNESent)   becoming young

"Because most people want to be **juvenescent**, elixirs and snake oils have been popular."

The *ju* part of this word comes from the Indo-European root, *ieu* (young). That root has given us "**ju**venile" and "**youth**."

K

kachina (kuCHĒnu) spirit ancestors, among Pueblo Indians; doll made of wood representing the spirit ancestors of Pueblo Indians

"Since he is one Pueblo Indian who doesn't believe in deifying ancestors or anyone else, he rejects the concept of **kachina**."

kakidrosis (kakiDRŌsis) body smell

"Take a shower every day to prevent **kakidrosis**."

kakistocracy (kakuSTOKrusē) government by the least capable or by the worst citizens

"The wealthy senator enjoys playing a role in America's plutocratic **kakistocracy**, where the incompetent rulers are usually well-to-do."

The *ka* sound in "kakistocracy" is the same sound found in "defe**ca**te." It's not too difficult to see how *caca*, the ancient word, as well as the baby-talk word, for "defecate" has also taken the meaning of "bad." From it, we also get "**cac**ophony," (literally, bad sound) and two other words in this dictionary: "**cac**ography" and "Kalli**kak**."

kakorrhaphiophobia   (KAK*oru* • FĒō • FŌbēu)   fear of failure

  " 'He who is down need not fear a fall' is at times quoted by those who have **kakorrhaphiophobia**."

kaleidogyn   (kuLĪdujin)   a beautiful woman

  "My friend argued that Raquel Welch was the quint-essential **kaleidogyn**."

Kallikak   (KALukak)   fictitious name of a family that exhibited high intelligence and achievement in one branch and mental deficiency and immorality in another branch

  "The discrepancies between the achievers and non-achievers in that family are so great that you'd swear that they were the **Kallikaks**."

  Kallikak is a fictitious surname given to a real family. The pseudonym may be considered an oxymoron (see entry), for it means literally good (*kalli*, as in "**calli**graphy"—beautiful handwriting) and bad (*kak*, as in "**cac**ophony"—bad sound). See also "dyscalligynia" and all words beginning with *caco-* and *kaki-*.

kleptocracy   (klepTOKrusē)   government by thieves

"She said that those government officials in charge of overseeing savings and loans were running a **kleptocracy**."

knickknackatory (nikNAKut*or*ē) a storehouse of knickknacks

"She reached into her **knickknackatory** and pulled out a useless ornament."

"Knickknack" is essentially a reduplication of the word "knack." Having a knack for something often indicates an ability to solve certain problems cleverly, hence sometimes to invent ingenious devices—"knacks" or, later, "knickknacks."

konimeter (kōNIMut*er*) an instrument for measuring dust in the air

"When we started coughing from all the dust, we pulled out a **konimeter**, which indicated that our cabin was much dustier than we had realized."

kratogen (KRATujin) a dormant area adjacent to one beset by earthquakes

"They were safe during the earthquake because they happened to be in a **kratogen** far away from the epicenter."

"We are situated, in a sense, in a **kratogen**, where in spite of all the earth's rumblings and troubles we somehow remain unaffected and immune to all of it."

Kriegspiel (KREEGSpēl) a game in which pieces representing military units are maneuvered on maps

"Because he was an extremely peace-loving and antimilitary man, he didn't want to play **Kriegspiel**, which he believed trivialized the destructiveness of war."

L

latebricole   (laTEBrikōl)   hiding or living in holes

"Since Bugs Bunny is a **latebricole** cartoon figure, you could fall into his house—if, of course, you were also a cartoon figure."

latifundian   (latiFUNdēun)   rich in real estate

"Despite his debts, Donald Trump owns some extremely valuable New York real estate, which qualifies him as **latifundian**."

The *fundi* part of this word refers to a landed estate or, literally, the bottom. The connection between land, bottom, and *fund* many not be readily apparent, but here goes: *fund* is related to the *fund* in such words as "**fund**amental" and "**found**ation," both of which pertain to that which is at the beginning, or the bottom. And the foundation of a house is located at its bottom—on the land, that is. You may also have heard of bottomland, which is low-lying land. Further, "bottom" and *fund* are themselves related in origin: Indo-European *bhudh* became *pythmen* in Greek, *fundus* in Latin, and *botn* in Old Norse, all relatives of English.

latitudinarian (LAtuT*U*duNERēun) a person having broad, free, and flexible views, especially about religion

"Far from being doctrinaire, he has been criticized by some for being too much of a **latitudinarian**."

latrability (lātruBILutē) the ability to bark

"Since our dog virtually never barked, we asked the vet whether **latrability** is essential to canine health."

law of recency (RĒsensē) the generalization holding that the more recent the item, event, or experience, the better it is remembered

"Because of the **law of recency**, I suggest that you mention your most important points at the end of your speech if you want your audience to remember them."

law of exercise the principle that repetition of an act promotes learning and makes subsequent performance of that act easier, other things being equal

"When concert pianists practice eight or nine hours a day, they are taking advantage of the **law of exercise**."

Lebensraum (LĀbunzr*ou*m) the freedom and space required or claimed by a person or a nation to achieve full development

"Hitler claimed that the Germans needed Poland and other lands for **Lebensraum**."

Lebensraum is the German word for "living space"— *leben* (life) plus *Raum* (space). The Nazis often used the term to imply that the territory they seized and held was necessary for the economic self-sufficiency of the German people. Today the term can be used to denote to any space required by a community, institution, organism, or individual for life, growth, or activity.

lilas (LĒlu)   Buddhist term for the futile pursuit of triviality

"In Buddhist terms, Thoreau rejected **lilas** in favor of the pursuit of what was truly valuable."

lipolysis (lĭPOlusis)   decomposition of fat

"By taking certain amino acids and doing various exercises, I hope to encourage **lipolysis** and so lose weight."

lirp (lerp)   to snap one's fingers

"The jazz musician would **lirp** so loud that we wondered whether he hurt his finger and thumb."

logamnesia (LAWGamnēzyu)   forgetting words

"With his huge vocabulary and quick mind, William F. Buckley doesn't have to worry about **logamnesia**."

logamnosis (lawgamNŌsis)   mania for trying to recall forgotten words

"There I was speaking before an audience of hundreds, yet fully engaged in **logamnosis**, struggling to recall what had been written on my stolen notes."

"Logamnosis" is composed of four roots: *log* (word), *a* (not), *mn* (memory), and *osis* (condition). The *mn* root occurs in a number of words relating to memory, including three other entries in this dictionary: "log**amn**esia," "**mn**emonics," and "paleo**mn**esia."

logophagist (lōGOfujist)   one who eats his or her own words

"When former President Bush reneged on his tax pledge, he became a **logophagist**."

longanimity (*law*nguNIMutē)   suffering in silence

"We are impressed that she bears her trials and misfortunes with **longanimity**."

lotic (LŌtik)   pertaining to or living in rapidly moving currents of water

"Some fish are **lotic** and are found only in streams, while others are lentic and are found in lakes."

lubber-wort (LUB*er* • wort)   food that has little or no nutritional value

"A chocolate chip cookie is an excellent example of **lubber-wort**."

lucubration (*lu*kyuBRĀshun)   late night study, especially by lamplight

"His **lucubration** for his bar exam resulted in tired eyes."

lugubrious (luGUBrēus)   mournful in an exaggerated or affected manner

"The actress's overwrought portrayal of the bereaved woman bordered on the **lugubrious**."

lurgulary (LERgyu • lerē)   the act of poisoning water

"Although there was no factual basis for the charge, medieval Jews were at times accused of poisoning wells, an action that involves a species of **lurgulary**."

lychnobite (LIKnubīt)   one who works at night and sleeps in the day

"Like many other **lychnobites** who work the graveyard shift, she has trouble getting adequate restorative sleep."

lysis (LĪsis)   the final phase of a disease

"We were happy to see the **lysis** of his fever."

M

malinger (muLING*er*)   to feign illness or incapacity in order to avoid duty or work

"He wasn't **malingering** to get out of his assignment; the student really was ill."

malneirophrenia (malnīrōFRĒNyu)   a disturbed state of mind following an unpleasant dream

"I awoke in a cold sweat, apparently in a **malneirophrenia**, shaking at the thought of what I had just dreamed."

mammothrept (MAmōthrept)   a child raised by its grandmother; a spoiled child

"After his mother and father died, the boy became a **mammothrept**."

managed (MANujd) **text**   a textbook written by freelancers or graduate students but credited to an individual, usually a professor, who only oversees and reviews its writing

"We consider **managed texts**, fairly common in the academic world, exploitation of graduate students, who receive no public acknowledgment for their writing."

marasmic (muRAZmik), **marantic** (muRANtik) of a wasting of the body, especially in the young because of malnutrition

"When they saw the thin, **marasmic** children in Somalia, the soldiers couldn't help being moved."

martingale (MAWRtingāl) gambling system in which one doubles the stakes to recover previous losses

"The gambler believed that by using a **martingale** tack he'd eventually win and recover all his losses."

mataeotechny (MAtēōTEKnē) an unprofitable art or science

"Woodcarving was a **mataeotechny** in which he engaged for the pure joy of it."

matutine (MACHutin) relating to the early morning

"I enjoy taking **matutine** walks before breakfast at 6:30 A.M.."

matutolypea (maTUtō • LIPēu) the condition of or act of getting up on the wrong side of the bed

"Did his unpleasant demeanor begin with **matutolypea**, or did it occur hours after he got out of bed?"

mazotropism (MĀzō·truPIZ′m) the influence or attraction that female breasts exert on a man

"It is impossible for most males to think of Dolly Parton without thinking of the power of **mazotropism**."

metrona (meTRŌNu) a young grandmother

"Because she gave birth when she was only sixteen and her daughter gave birth at roughly the same age, she became a **metrona** at thirty-two."

miasma (mīAZmu) a dangerous, corrupting, or deceiving influence or atmosphere

"I always find myself in a **miasma** of cigarette smoke."

The root of "miasma" is *mai* (to stain or defile). This root has given us also "**mia**smology" (the study of pollution), "**Mia**stor" (a genus of flies, which often carry germs), "**a**mianthus" (a type of asbestos that fire cannot defile), and possibly "**m**ole," a defilement of the skin.

At one time, "miasma" denoted a poisonous atmosphere that was thought to rise from swamps and decaying matter and to cause disease.

Micawberish (miCAWberish) optimistic, like Mr. Micawber, a character in Dickens's *David Copperfield*, who always trusted that something good would turn up

"We need to take action and not rely on a passive, **Micawberish** hopefulness."

microlipet (mīkrōLIPut) someone who is bothered by trifles

"A **microlipet** with a tendency toward irrational behavior could easily succumb to violent impulses over the most insignificant events."

micrology (mīKROLujē) excessive devotion to details

"We need to keep in mind our important goals and not become sidetracked by **micrology**."

microphonia (MĪkrō • FONēu) a weak, hardly audible voice

"He'll never be a dynamic speaker unless he speaks up and overcomes his **microphonia**."

misandry (MISandrē) hatred of men

"Since many lesbians form close friendships with males, they shouldn't be accused of **misandry**."

misapodysis (MISupōDISis) hatred of undressing in front of someone

"His commanding officer explained to him that he must overcome his **misapodysis** if he is to live in close quarters with other men."

The *dy* part of this word comes from the Indo-European root, *do* (to give). It has evolved into the English words "**do**nate," "**da**te" (a given point in time), "Tra**d**e," "tradition" (handed down to subsequent generations), "**da**ta" (given information), "ad**d**" and "e**d**ition" (including that which is added up, given, or given up), "surren**d**er" (giving oneself up), "ren**t**" and "ren**d**er" (give up, yield), "anti**d**ote" (a remedy given to the sick), "anec**d**ote" (literally, not given out—unpublished, that is), and the names **D**orothea and Theo**d**ore (gift of God), Isi**d**ore (gift of Isis), and Eu**d**ora (good gift).

The *do* root has given us "en**d**ysis" (the process of growing—being given—new hair), "**d**off" (to "do off"—remove, that is), "ec**d**ysis" (removal of the skin, molting), "ec**d**ysiast" (stripteaser), and "a**d**ytum" (a temple in which laypersons may not [*a*-] enter, but priests may enter—presumably to *give* sacrifices).

miscorrection (miskuREKshun) a new error made in the course of correcting an old one

"I gave other people the task of correcting her errors, since I knew that she was likely to introduce **miscorrections**."

misfeasance (misFĒz′nts) a lawful act performed in an unlawful way

"Because the politician gave special privileges to a corporation in which he owned stock, he is now vulnerable to the charge of **misfeasance**."

misocainia (misōKĪnēu) the hatred of anything new or strange, as in new ideas

"Beware of **misocainia**, since most currently acceptable ideas were unpopular when they were new."

misocapnist (mīsōKAPnist)   one who hates tobacco smoke; a hater of smoking

"King James I criticized tobacco so severely that he has become one of the most famous **misocapnists**."

misogamist (miSOGumist)   one who hates marriage

"Even though the philosopher Immanuel Kant never married, he was no **misogamist**."

mnemonic (nēMONik)   aiding memory

"The word 'HOMES' is an excellent **mnemonic** device for remembering the five Great Lakes."

modus vivendi (MŌdus • viVENdē)   a temporary arrangement between persons or parties pending a settlement of matters in debate

"Until the divorce is settled, we need to reach a **modus vivendi** so that we won't be constantly fighting."

moirologist (moyROLujist)   a hired mourner

"Since she thought that all mourners should be sincere and unpaid, she couldn't condone the use of **moirologists**."

"Although they didn't like the man enough to attend his funeral, they did like him enough to chip in for a **moirologist**."

Moloch (MOluk)   a system, method, or power that requires human sacrifice

"She was happy to be through with the **Moloch**, which was how she described the torturous grind of law school."

molysmophobia (MOlismō·FŌbēu), **mysophobia** (mīsuFŌbēu)   fear of dirt or contamination

"The rich and famous Howard Hughes had **molysmophobia** so severely that, to avoid germs, he was reputed to heat up newspapers in ovens before reading them."

monepic (MONupik) consisting of one word, or of one-word sentences

"Her **monepic** but effective reply was 'Never!'"

mot propre (mō·proPUR)   the correct or necessary word

"She was happy when she lit upon the *mot propre* for the practice she was trying to describe."

mucker pose (MUK*er*·pōz)   a pretense of ignorance or uncultivated tastes, often used in an attempt to appear humble

"When Senator Sam Ervin, who was a Harvard Law School graduate and the chair of the committee investigating the Watergate affair, referred to himself as a simple old country lawyer, he was affecting a **mucker pose**."

mullion (MULyun) window bar

"The **mullions** that covered the windows ostensibly to keep criminals from breaking in were only window dressing, for in reality the criminals—white-collar criminals—were already inside."

mullock (MULuk) **tailing** (TĀLing) mining refuse

"The miners tried to be especially surefooted around the **mullock**."

The *mull* in this word is directly related to the *mull*ing many of us are doing as we read this book—mulling it over. Figuratively we flip things over and around and pull them apart—that is, we *grind* things up—in our minds. And that is the meaning of the original Indo-European root of *mull*: *mel*, meaning "grind." From it we get "**mo**lar" (a tooth that grinds food), "**mill**" (which grinds), "**meal**" (which has been ground), "**mal**t," "**mill**et," "**mael**strom," and "**mol**d" (ground or molded into shape). Now that we've **mull**ed that over, we can remove the chaff and leave it for the collector of our minds' refuse.

multivocal (multēVOKul) a single word having a variety of meanings or connotations

"The word 'set' is so multivocal as to be the longest entry in my dictionary."

multivocality (MULtē•vōKALitē) a variety of meanings or senses

"The biblical scholar insisted that the concept of the Messiah had such **multivocality** for the ancient Hebrews that many disagreed on who or what a Messiah was or would be."

mumpsimus (MUMPsumus) a prejudice commonly adhered to in spite of evidence; also one who holds a mumpsimus

"A blindly held belief is often a **mumpsimus**, in which no amount of evidence will shake one's faith."

mundivagant (munDIVigunt) wandering over the world

"Prejudice is, sadly, a thoroughly **mundivagant** phenomenon that has, in one form or other, permeated almost every society on the globe."

mundungus (munDUNGus) the stench of tobacco

"As she opened the door to the smoke-filled room, she was nearly overcome by the **mundungus** and quickly turned back."

natalitious   (nātuLISHus)   pertaining to one's birthday

"She dislikes any **natalitious** celebrations, since they remind her of her advancing age."

naufragous   (NAWFrugus)   causing shipwrecks

"No ship's captain doubts that icebergs are **naufragous**."

naumachy   (NAWm'kē)   a naval battle

"The **naumachy** between the *Monitor* and the *Merrimack* is famous."

necromimesis   (nekrō • miMĒsis)   playing dead

"The wounded man, who appeared to be dead to the enemy soldiers, was saved from death because of his **necromimesis**."

The *nec* part of this word comes from the Indo-European root, *nek*, meaning "damage" or "destroy." The root is related to, though somewhat stronger than, the *ne* root in such words as "**ne**gative" and "**ana**rchy." It produced "**ne**cropolis" (cemetery—literally, a city of corpses), "**nui**sance," "in**noc**ent," and "**nec**tar" (originally the drink of the gods, who were immortal—that is, exempt from death).

nelipot (NELipot)   one who goes barefoot

"Concerned about sanitation and podobromhidrosis [see "podobromhidrosis"], the restaurant did not admit **nelipots**."

neologism (nēOLujiz′m)   a new word or a new meaning for an existing word

"Computers have inspired many **neologisms**, including the word 'byte.'"

nepenthe (niPEN[T]thē)   anything that brings forgetfulness of sorrow or suffering

"For many poor people, heroin is a **nepenthe**, with which they can escape—temporarily—their suffering."

nepheligenous (nefuLIJunus)   producing clouds of tobacco smoke

"**Nepheligenous** Mark Twain was often seen through clouds of cigar smoke."

nephometer (niFOMut*er*)   an instrument that measures the proportion of sky covered by cloud

"One doesn't need a **nephometer** to know when the sky is cloudy."

nomogamosis (numo·g′MŌsis) marriage between persons who are highly suitable for each other

"In their **nomogamosis**, each marital partner always gives encouragement to the other and always shows a willingness to understand and compromise."

nonce (nonts) **word** a word, usually short-lived, that is devised for a single occasion or publication

"The **nonce word** they coined fell into disuse within a month after it was introduced."

noodling (NUD′ling) music that is played as titles or credits roll

"I didn't leave until after the credits because I enjoyed listening to the **noodling**."

nosism (NŌsiz′m) use of "we" in speaking of oneself to suggest one's importance; group conceit

"Next time he wants to express his view he needs to own up to that view by using the pronoun 'I' instead of engaging in **nosism**."

The *nos* part of this word is an ancient remnant of the Indo-European root, *nes*, which has evolved into "us" (from Old English *uns*) and "our" (from Germanic *unsara* and Old English *user*), as well as "nostrum" (literally, our own—that is, made by the seller—a quack remedy, often with secret ingredients) and "Notre Dame" (French, "Our Lady," for the Virgin Mary). It is also the origin of the name Nostradamus—*Michel de Nostredame*.

nosocomephobia   (nōzō·kōmuFŌbēu)   fear of hospitals

"We weren't sure whether his discomfort at the hospital was due more to his illness or to his **nosocomephobia**."

nullipara   (nuLIPuru)   a woman who has borne no children

"Although she is still a **nullipara**, she wants to produce at least one child before she turns thirty."

numen   (N[Y]*U*min)   an inner guiding force or spirit

"Each person from that New Age group claimed to be influenced by a **numen**, which would direct his or her spiritual journey."

numerate   (N*U*Merut)   having the ability to read and understand numbers

"The alert, **numerate** accountant filled out the tax forms so quickly that my refund came almost before I stepped into his office."

nyctalopia   (niktuLŌpēu)   night blindness

"People who have **nyctalopia** should avoid driving at night."

nympholepsy   (NIM[P]fulepsē)   a state of ecstasy or frenzy caused by a desire for the unobtainable

"His unreasonable insistence that the world be exactly as he wished it to be had sent him into **nympholepsy**."

"Nymph" comes from the Indo-European root, *(s)neubh* (to marry). Nymphomania is excessive lustfulness in a woman. "Nympholepsy" originally referred to the ecstasy a man feels when he has caught a glimpse of a nymph—an unattainable female. Other English words from *sneubh* include "**nup**tials," "**nub**ile" (of marriageable age), and "con**nub**ial." (See also "a**nup**taphobia.")

O

obelize (OBulīz), **athetize**   to indicate (with, for example, a plus sign) that the succeeding text is doubtful or spurious

"The editors felt required to **obelize** the unverified quotations."

obsequiousness (ubSĒKwēusnes)   excessive compliance and service

"Servers at restaurants need to draw a line between cheerfully brisk and polite service, on the one hand, and **obsequiousness**, on the other."

obsidium (ubSIDēum)   a bout of sexual debauchery

"Although he enjoyed the **obsidium** while it lasted, it left him with a serious disease."

omnilegent (omNILujunt)   reading everything

"John Milton was **omnilegent**, reading deeply in several languages, including French, English, Italian, and the classical languages."

113

omniscient (omNISHunt)   knowing everything

"The theologian insisted on God's **omniscience** and argued against literal interpretations of the Bible according to which God is said to discover facts."

omnivorous (omNIV[u]rus)   eating, or devouring, of all kinds of foods; taking in everything indiscriminately, as with the mind

"His appetite for life was **omnivorous**, driving him constantly to take in new experiences."

one-trial learning   the total mastery of a skill on the first trial

"She was a brilliant student and was known for her **one-trial learning**."

oneirataxia (ōnīruTAKSēu)   the inability to differentiate between fantasy and reality

"Since almost 250,000 Americans wrote to the television character Dr. Marcus Welby to ask for medical advice, many Americans apparently suffer from **oneirataxia**."

oneirocritic (ōNĪrō • kritik)   one who specializes in the interpretation of dreams

"Although Freud claimed to be an **oneirocritic**, many people doubt whether dreams are as heavily symbolic and as precisely interpretable as he seemed to suggest."

oniomania (ōnēōMĀnēu) an irrepressible urge to buy things

"Anyone who has **oniomania** ought not to have a charge account."

onomatophobia (onu · matu · FŌbēu) fear of hearing a certain word or words

"The author held that the concept of blasphemy resulted from **onomatophobia**."

onomatopoeic (onu · matu · PĒik) pertaining to words formed from the sound they are intended to denote, as "meow" and "moo" represent the sounds made by cats and cows

"She enjoyed **onomatopoeic** words because she thought they were somehow closer to reality than other words."

opsomania (opsōMĀnēu) a craving for a particular food

"When her son demanded pizza and only pizza for dinner every evening, she asked him to get a grip on his **opsomania**."

optotype (OPtutīp) the wall chart used to test eyesight

"He memorized the letters on the **optotype** so that he could pass the eye test."

orgulous (ORGyulus) arrogantly proud

"One can have self-esteem without being **orgulous**."

oriflamme (*OR*uflam) a symbol that inspires devotion or courage, especially a banner that rallies troops in battle

"Just a glimpse of their **oriflamme** was sufficient for the soldiers to continue the battle in spite of the overwhelming odds against their winning."

orismology (*ori*zMOLuje̅) the science of defining technical terms

"Because linguistic clarity is essential to most technical fields, **orismology** demands exact definitions."

orogeny (*aw*ROJune̅) the process by which mountains are formed

"Since the geologist was raised in a mountainous country, he was especially interested in **orogeny**."

orometer (*aw*ROMut*er*) a type of barometer used for measuring the height of mountains

"Carefully planning your goals is the best **orometer** you can have for gauging seemingly mountainous challenges."

orthodromics (*or*thuDROMiks) sailing on a straight course

"Why should you take the tortuous route when **orthodromics** will get you there quickly and safely?"

oxter (*AWK*St*er*) to walk arm in arm; to put the arm around

"The man **oxtered** his wife's arm so that she could walk without falling down."

oxymoron (oksiMORon) contradictory words combined in one phrase, as in "the sounds of silence"

"The comedian pointed out that 'guest host' is an **oxymoron**."

This word is itself an oxymoron—a contradiction in terms, that is—for the two Greek roots of the word, *oxy* and *moron*, are contradictory. *Moron* means "foolish"—that is, not sharp, not smart. Yet *oxy* means "sharp" or "pointed." (See also "aculeate.") Thus, "oxymoron" literally means "pointedly foolish" or "sharply unsharp." (See "Kallikak," an example of an oxymoron.)

P

padrone (puDRŌNu) an employer who exploits his workers and virtually controls their lives, providing them with accommodations and food as well as employment

"At one time Italian immigrants were dependent on **padrones**, who would exploitatively employ them."

paedogenetic (pēdō • juNEDik) of animals that reproduce while in the larval state or in some other juvenile form

"Certain gall insects reproduce without having acquired adult characteristics and so are **paedogenetic**."

paleomnesia (pālēomNĒZyu) the condition of being able to remember events of the far past

"Elderly people, though often known for their **paleomnesia**, at times have trouble remembering the recent past."

paletoted (PALutōd) clothed in a loose garment such as a toga or a robe

"The toga-party scene in the movie *Animal House* is memorable for the performance of the **paletoted** John Belushi."

pansophy (PANsufē)   universal, all-embracing knowledge

"They were temperamentally opposed to comprehensive philosophical systems; they preferred accumulating truths piecemeal rather than constructing a **pansophy**."

parabiosis (parubīŌsis)   an artificial or natural union of the blood circulation of two individuals, as in Siamese twins

"The Siamese twins had come to accept their **parabiosis**."

parachronism (paRAKruniz'm)   an incorrect date

"When the student placed Custer's last stand before the Civil War, he quickly recognized the **parachronism**."

The *chron* (time, age) part of "parachronism" comes from an ancient root, *gher*, which meant "to seize, embrace, or enclose." "**Chor**us" comes from the same root, the connection being that the Greek *khoros* was an enclosed place for dancing. "**Surgeon**" comes to us by way of "**chirurgeon**," literally, "a hand worker," since the hand *encloses* things (see also "**chir**otony"). One can also see how **gir**dle, **gar**den, and **cour**tyard relate to enclosure.

How, though, you ask, does the root *chrono* relate to time or dates? Simple: time has been regarded as that which embraces all things. Thus, the ancient *gher* (embrace) root gave rise to the Greek word *khronos*, which gives us *chrono*.

paradigmatic (perudigMATik)   pertaining to the determination of a word's meaning by examining the word itself rather than by considering it in the context of the sentence

"Far from being **paradigmatic**, most of the words in Berent and Evans's dictionary require clear definitions and, in some cases, even example sentences, such as this one, for the words to be adequately understood."

paragenital　(peruJENit´l)　preventing conception during intercourse

"**Paragenital** intercourse, whether involving the diaphragm or other barrier methods, is forbidden by his religion."

paralipophobia　(peru•lipō•FŌbēu)　fear of neglecting a duty

"So conscientious was she in discharging her duties that we thought that she had **paralipophobia**."

parley　(PAWRlē)　a discussion of points in dispute, as an informal conference to arrange peace terms

"Democratic and Republican leaders must conduct several **parleys** if they are ever to design effective legislation to reduce the national debt."

paroemiology　(puRĒmēolujē)　the technique or practice of coining proverbs

"Ralph Waldo Emerson, one of the most widely quoted writers in English, was adept at **paroemiology**."

parturient　(pawrTERēunt)　about to give birth; about to produce an idea or discovery

"Socrates regarded himself as an intellectual midwife who would elicit ideas from his interlocutors' **parturient** minds."

parvenu (P*AWR*ven*u*) a newly rich or powerful person

"People may say that I'm a **parvenu**, but my newfound riches are of the spirit, not material wealth."

pasilaly (PASi·lālē) a universal language

"Love is a true **pasilaly**; unfortunately, it seems that hate may be one too."

passe-partout (pasp*er*T*U*) a universal pass or means of entry; a master key

"Her kindness was her **passe-partout**, which could unlock any door—or any heart."

patavinity (padu VINitē) the use of local words, expressions, or pronunciations

"Without her fluent **patavinity**, she could never have gained the trust of the natives."

"Patavinity" comes from the Italian place-name Patavium, now known as Padua. It was in Padua that the Roman historian Livy (Titus Livius) was born, and it was in Livy's writings from the first century B.C. that the distinctive dialect of Padua was recorded.

patellar (puTEL*er*) **reflex** spontaneous forward extension of the lower leg elicited by a sudden sharp tap against the patellar tendon, just below the kneecap

"When she called him a hurtful name, we knew that he'd lose his temper just as certainly as a tap below the knee would activate the **patellar reflex**."

penelopize (piNELupīz) to stall for time by redoing something

"If he continued to **penelopize**, people would either grow tired of his repetitive actions or realize that he was stalling for time."

peneplain, peneplane (PĒnēplān) an area of land made almost level by long-continued erosion

"With any further erosion, the **peneplain** would become flat."

pentheraphobia (PENth*eru* • FŌbēu) fear of one's mother-in-law

"Did his passive body language while he was near his mother-in-law reflect **pentheraphobia** or simply a desire to avoid an argument?"

The *ther* part of this word is probably related to the *ther* in "theravada" (speech of the elders). The root derives from Sanskrit *sthavira* (stout, old, or venerable), from which we have "steer," "taurus" (bull), "Minotaur," and "toreador," all of which some (of the more vicious sorts) would say are appropriate synonyms for "mother-in-law."

penultima (piNULtimu) a woman who freely indulges in sex play but stops short of the last act

"He regarded Madonna as a **penultima**, tantalizing her viewers without going all the way."

penultimate (piNULtumut) pertaining to that which is next to last

"She made her point in the **penultimate** paragraph, then used the final paragraph simply to thank those who had helped her write the essay."

peribolos, peribolus (puRIBulus) a wall around sacred ground

"The man was certain that the **peribolos** around the church cemetery would keep out evil."

phagocytose (FAGuciTŌS) in biology, to engulf or absorb (a cell or particle) like a phagocyte (blood cell that engulfs and destroys foreign particles in the blood), so as to isolate and destroy it.

"In a debate, the skilled polemicist **phagocytosed** his inexperienced opponents."

phaneromania (FANerōMĀnēu) the habit of picking at scabs, biting one's nails, or poking at pimples

"One of their friends had a bloody arm from his **phaneromania**."

A phantom is something falsely revealed—an illusion. A phanerogam is a plant having visible, exposed reproductive organs (as opposed to a cryptogam). Phanerozoic animals are those that live on the earth's surface and hence are

123

exposed. An epiphany is a sudden enlightenment, and a theophany is a manifestation of a god. So you can see now why the *phanero* part of "phaneromania" pertains to things like scabs, nails, and pimples, for all those things are on the surface of the skin—obvious, exposed, "easy pickings."

By the way, *phaner* is also related to "banner" (which is meant to be seen), "bandits" (who appear suddenly), and the numerous *photo-* words that pertain to light (which reveals a great deal).

pharology (fāROLujē) the science of signal lights and lighthouses

"In the study of **pharology** one learns the exact light signals with which to communicate to ships."

phatic (FATĭk) pertaining to speech that is meant to express friendship or sociability rather than to convey information

"The linguist explained to us that the question 'How are you?' is usually a form of stroking and has a **phatic** rather than an informative function."

phenotype (FĒNutīp) the observable characteristics of an individual resulting from the interaction of inherited genes and environment

"The man, who grew up in Beverly Hills and whose father and grandfather were famous actors, was virtually destined to acquire the **phenotype** of an entertainer."

philemyosis filu • miŌSis) kissing while the eyes are closed

"When I am expected to kiss someone I find unattractive, I compromise by practicing **philemyosis**, so that I don't have to see the person."

phlangonologist (flanjuNOLujist)   collector of dolls

"The **phlangonologist** had every Barbie doll ever made."

phonaesthesia (fōnisTHĒZyu)   the phenomenon of certain word elements' seeming to have an innate meaning or flavor—for example: *st*, which suggests fixity, as in "stone" and "stiff"; *sl*, a gliding sound, as in "slither," "slobber," "slide," and "slope"; and *gl*, a shining quality, as in "glow," "gleam," and "glimmer"

"It was **phonaesthesia** at first hearing, for he was in love and even the name Tallulah seemed to fit perfectly the description of his dream date."

phosphorescence (fawsfuRESunts)   the property of continuing to shine in the dark after exposure to light

"The lone rational voice among the lynch mob was like a small patch of **phosphorescence** in an otherwise dark room."

"The things he learned that day would stay with him for the rest of his life, remaining **phosphorescent** long afterward."

photobiotic (FŌtō・bīoTik)   requiring light to live or thrive

"Many plants are **photobiotic** and will die if they are regularly deprived of light."

photolysis (fōTOLusis) the breakdown of substances due to the presence of light

"Bringing the abuses to light, rather than hiding them in the closet, would cause them to be dealt with and soon destroyed, the objects of **photolysis**."

photopathy (fōTOPuthē) the movement of a cell or organism in response to, and usually away from, the light

"His contempt for ideas—his **photopathy**, if you will—is so strong that he refuses to be enlightened."

pilpul (PILpul) a thorough, hair-splitting argument, especially among Jewish Talmudic scholars

"He wasn't about to get into a **pilpul** with the rabbi, since he didn't believe in most of the Old Testament anyway."

pismirism (PISmir·iz'm) petty saving

"She rationalized that her coupon-clipping mania and her **pismirism** would ensure for her child the things she never had when she was young."

plutocracy (pluTOKrusē) government by the wealthy

"Considering the fact that the president, the vice president, and virtually all members of Congress are from the upper classes, many would argue that the United States government is a **plutocracy**."

Plutus was, in Greek myth, the god of wealth.

podobromhidrosis (POdōbrōm • hiDRŌsis)   smelly feet

"Your friends won't tell you that you have **podobromhidrosis**; they'll just say, 'Your feet stink.'"

poliosis (pōlēŌSis)   premature graying of the hair

"The gray-haired man, who was only thirty, says that **poliosis** runs in his family."

pollard (POLurd)   an animal bereft of its horns

"Without his speechwriters and comedy writers, the entertainer was virtually powerless—a **pollard**, hornless and no longer majestic."

poncif (PAWNsif)   a hackneyed notion or expression offered with an air of authority or originality

"As if he had just discovered a new chemical element, he offered the following **poncif** for our enlightenment: 'You gotta have money to make money.'"

pone (PŌne; pōn)   player on dealer's right who cuts cards

"Since he was on the dealer's right, he was the **pone** and so had the honor of cutting the cards."

pons asinorum (PONZ as′NORum)   a crucial and critical test; something difficult for the uninitiated to understand or grasp

"The series of tests she took for Mensa, the high-IQ society, was a **pons asinorum**, designed to weed out most people."

pornogenarian (PORno • jiNERēun)   a dirty old man

"When Hugh Hefner married a woman several years his junior, he was considered a **pornogenarian**."

pornopatch (PORno • pach)   a gratuitous passage of explicit sex inserted in a novel by an author or editor to give the book more selling appeal

"The editor demanded a **pornopatch** from the novelist, but the novelist insisted on including only those sex scenes that were integral to the novel."

porrect (puREKT)   to stretch out horizontally

"If he goes into the ring with Tyson, Tyson will **porrect** him."

potvaliant (potVALyunt)   courage produced by drunkenness

"We were afraid that if they had too much to drink they would become **potvaliant** and lose their jobs for telling off their supervisors."

preagonal (prēAGun′l)   just before death

"His strange **preagonal** request was that he be buried in his car."

preantepenultimate (prēANtē•penULtimut) the one before the one before the next to the last (fourth from last)

"Everybody knows that *w* is the **preantepenultimate** letter in our alphabet."

prescind (prēSIND) to consider individually, to separate in thought, or to detach oneself

"In looking at their theory, we need to **prescind** the important principles from any insignificant details in which those principles are embedded."

prolegomena (proluGOMunu) long introductions

"I skipped over the **prolegomena** and went straight to the author's main thesis."

prolepsis (prōLEPsis) the anticipation of possible arguments or objections so that they can be neutralized or disposed of before the opposition has a chance to use them.

"When the speaker began by saying, 'Some people have raised an objection,' we knew she was about to introduce a **prolepsis**."

prosopography (prosōPOGrufē) vivid description of a person or character

"The novelist was so adept at **prosopography** that her readers thought that some of her characters were real."

prosopolepsy (pruSŌPulepsē)   a partiality for someone based primarily on the person's looks

"Psychologists have demonstrated that **prosopolepsy** operates even as early as kindergarten, where good-looking children are likely to receive preferential treatment."

pro tanto (prōTANtō)   to some extent; for what it's worth

"I can support your decision **pro tanto** but not with complete enthusiasm."

psaphonic (saFONik)   planning one's rise to fame

"Using his **psaphonic** mind, he planned systematically to write down his goals and the steps to achieve them."

psellismophobia (seLIZmō • FŌbēu)   fear of stuttering

"When he sang, he neither stuttered nor felt anxious over the possibility of stuttering; it was as if his **psellismophobia** had temporarily disappeared."

pseudogyny (suDOJinē)   the adoption of the woman's name by a man at the time of marriage

"In this culture, many men would consider **pseudogyny** only if their wives' names were much more famous than their own."

psomophagy (sōMOFujē)   swallowing food without thorough chewing

"If you want to remain healthy, you'll need to chew your food thoroughly and avoid **psomophagy**."

ptarmic   (TAWRmik)   likely to cause sneezing

"Pepper blown into the face can be **ptarmic**."

ptochocracy   (tōKOKrusē)   government by the poor

"I oppose both plutocracy and **ptochocracy** and favor instead a government ruled by the best-qualified leaders, whether they are rich or poor."

ptochogony   (tōKOGunē)   a system that produces poverty

"Many Republican politicians argue that the welfare system is a **ptochogony**, guaranteeing the perpetuation of poverty."

pudendojacosis   (pyuDENdō • juKOSis)   the thrusting forward of the genitals, as in a striptease

"The minister exhorted his parishioners to develop an interest in ballet and classical dance and warned against an obsessive interest in rock music and the **pudendojacosis** characteristic of those who dance to it."

puff   (puf)   undue praise

"**Puff** may be good for promotional purposes but to keep people buying products, one must satisfy the customers."

pugil (PY*U*jil) a pinch that can be held between the thumb and first two fingers

"You may have a **pugil** of this cookie but not a bit more."

punctatim (punkTĀtim) point for point

"She systematically responded to his objections **punctatim**."

Q

quaestuary   (KWESchuwerē)   done for money

"The economist emphasized that **quaestuary** actions are vital to a healthy economy."

qualtagh   (KWOLtok)   the first person one sees after leaving the house

"Ironically, when he left the house the **qualtagh** was his ex-wife, whom he hadn't seen in twenty years."

querent   (KWIRunt)   one who consults an astrologer

"Long interested in astrology, Nancy Reagan was one of the country's most prominent **querents**."

quiddity   (KWIDitē)   the essence of a thing

"Socrates wanted to know the essence—the **quiddity**—of holiness."

Quinapalus   (KwinAPulus)   an authority cited to clinch an argument

"During the medieval period, a biblical character or Aristotle was often cited as a **Quinapalus** to win an argument."

quonking (KWONKing) noises picked up by a microphone or camera on a television or radio show

"Nowadays, the noisy, vulgar hosts and the equally noisy, vulgar guests are worse than the **quonking**—or they *are* the **quonking**."

R

rack rent (RAK • rint) exorbitant rent

"The slumlord had no qualms about charging **rack rent** for buildings that should have been condemned long ago."

rasorial (ruSORēul) habitually scratching the ground for food

"Chickens are **rasorial** birds, always searching for food on the ground."

reify (RĒufī) to convert an abstraction—for example, a plan or a dream—into a concrete thing; to talk about an abstraction as if it were a concrete thing

"Let us **reify** this dream so that one day 'prejudice' and 'bigotry' will be obsolete words."

The *re* in "reify" is related to the *re* in the Latin phrase "in re," which is another way of saying, "in the matter of." For "*res*" is the Latin word for "matter," a thing, that is. It is also very much the **r**eal thing, "real" being another word originating from *re*. Note also that "republic" comes from the phrase, *res publica*, literally, "public thing(s)" or "public wealth."

remontant (riMAWNtunt)   flowering more than once in a season, as do certain roses

"While her earlier performances were called the best of the season, we're certain that she is **remontant** and will soon flower again."

resipiscent (resuPISunt)   learned from experience

"His knowledge of the value of hard work was thoroughly **resipiscent,** gained from more than thirty years of working in the mines."

resupination (rēsupuNĀshun)   the act of lying on the back; or turning to an upside-down position

"I didn't want to cause you to arise, since you seemed deeply relaxed in your **resupination**."

resurrectionist (rezuREKshunist)   a body thief

"The **resurrectionists** then sold the body parts to medical corporations."

retiary (RĒshē•erē)   using a net

"The **retiary** rescue workers were ready for the man to jump."

retroussé   (retru̱SĀ)   turned up at the tip, as a nose

"Her **retroussé** nose gave her an impish look."

revenant   (REVununt)   one who has returned after a long absence; remembering something long forgotten

"When he came home after spending six years abroad, he was a most welcome **revenant**."

rived   (RĪVd)   split, not sawed

"He was like wood that had been **rived** out rather than sawed neatly or carefully chiseled, for his strength and durability came from hard experience, not from formal training or a carefully followed plan."

roorback   (RORbak)   a false report circulated to damage the reputation of a political candidate

"Ross Perot submitted that he was a victim of **roorbacks** circulated by some Republicans who were in charge of dirty tricks."

Rorschach   (RORshok)   psychological test in which the subject must tell the examiner what various inkblots look like to him

"He was so ugly that his self-portrait looked more like a **Rorschach test** than a person's face."

roundel   (ROUNd'l)   round window

"The sailor loved looking through the **roundel**, since it reminded him of the portholes on his ship."

rusticate (RUStiKāt) to go to the country

"He left New York City to **rusticate** in an almost uninhabited part of Vermont."

S

sabaist (SĀbāist) worshiper of stars

"I'm not a **sabaist**, but I do believe in astrology."

saccade (saKĀD) the rapid jump made by the eye as it shifts from one object to another

"We noticed his frequent **saccades**, which led us to believe that he didn't want us to think we were being spied upon."

saprophilous (suPROFulus) thriving in decaying matter

"The politician referred to the pornographer as 'a **saprophilous**, fimetarious maggot.'"

scissel (SISul) the scraps of metal plate left over from the process of minting coins

"At the rate of the devaluing of the dollar, coins will hardly be worth as much as their **scissel**."

scofflaw (SKOF*law*) a person who habitually breaks the law

"The politician pronounced curses on ne'er-do-wells, vagrants, and **scofflaws**."

scotoma (skuTŌMu) a blind spot

"Often even typically unprejudiced persons block out those ideas that run counter to their experiences, creating figurative **scotomas** that only knowledge and open-mindedness can clear up."

scotophobia (skōtōFŌbēu) fear of darkness

"They wanted night-lights because of their **scotophobia**."

scotopia (skuTŌPēu) the ability to see in dim light

"In darker times, people need a kind of **scotopia**, an ability to see even when the accepted fallacies and prejudices of their day threaten to blind them."

scree (skrē) mountain rubble

"The mountaineers needed to be careful as they approached the **scree** at the base of the cliff."

screed (skrēd) a long and tiresome speech

"The politician's almost endless **screed** put several people to sleep."

scribacious (skriBĀshus) given to or fond of writing

"Any author who writes more than twenty books *must* be **scribacious**."

scripturient (skripTYERēent) having a great urge to write or to be an author (a more positive version of "scribacious")

"With undiminished eagerness, the **scripturient** author wrote twelve hours a day until she finished her novel."

scunner (SKUNer) an unreasonable dislike

"She took a **scunner** at her former boyfriend's new girlfriend."

serendipity (serunDIPuty) a lucky discovery made accidentally

"His discovery of the vaccine was sheer **serendipity**."

This word was formed from the Persian fairy tale *The Three Princes of Serendib*. The princes had this accidental good fortune. Serendib was the Arab name of an island better known today as Ceylon or Sri Lanka. The Arab name was based, quite weakly, on the Sanskrit name for the island, Simhaladvipa, meaning Dwelling-Place-of-Lions Island.

seriatim (sirēĀdim) in series; one at a time

"When he mentioned all the benefits **seriatim**, we couldn't resist the insurance policy."

sermocination (sermosinĀshun) quickly answering one's own question

"Because of his **sermocinations**, there was little opportunity for debate."

serotinous (suROT′nus)   late blossoming

"Some people, like some plants, are **serotinous**, but they look great once they do bloom."

sesquipedalian (seskwipuDĀLyun)   using long words

"When I told her she was **sesquipedalian**, she replied, 'No, not at all; I'm an octogenarian.'"

Sherman (SHERmun) **statement**   the supposedly final and irrevocable, but usually untrue, statement by a politician that he or she will not run for office.

"We don't take seriously any politician's **Sherman statement**."

sidereal (SIDerul)   determined by the stars

"Our future is not **sidereal** but dependent on us."

sigmoidal (sigMOId′l)   curved in two directions

"The letter *s*, like some serpentine streets, is **sigmoidal**."

signpost (SĪN • pōst) **writing**   the overuse, in writing, of references such as "abovementioned," "former," "latter," and "discussed below."

"Her essay is so full of references to itself that it is the worst example of **signpost writing** I've ever seen."

smell-feast   (SMELfēst)   an uninvited dinner guest

"We have sufficient food for our invited guests, but not enough for **smell-feasts**."

snuffle   (SNUF'l)   to breathe noisily, as when a dog follows a scent

"We weren't sure whether he **snuffled** because he smelled something or whether he simply had a cold."

soceraphobia   (SŌsuruFŌbēu)   fear or dislike of one's in-laws

"His mother-in-law's pushiness and inconsiderateness were the primary causes of his **soceraphobia**."

sockdolager   (sokDOLuj*er*)   a decisive blow or answer that settles a dispute

"After looking up the answer in the *Guinness Book of World Records*, he delivered the **sockdolager**."

solifidian   (soluFIDēun)   one who believes that faith alone, without achievement or personal merit, will lead to salvation

"Unlike some **solifidian** Protestant soteriologies [views on salvation], Catholic doctrine holds that both faith and good works are required for salvation."

Some Christians, especially Protestants, have claimed that the letters of Saint Paul support the conviction that merely believing certain tenets of Christianity is sufficient for salvation.

soliloquial (suLILukwul) talking to oneself

"My **soliloqual** conversations help me concentrate and solve problems."

solipsism (SOLip • siz′m) the theory or belief that the only thing that exists is oneself, that all other reality is merely subjective

"I find it silly that some philosophers try to convince *other people* of the truth of **solipsism**."

spindle (SPINd′l) a measure of length of yarn

"The unsuccessful fisherman will pay out quite a few **spindles** before he's finished weaving this yarn."

spit (spit) to rain briefly

"We didn't bring umbrellas, since we were sure that it would only **spit**; we never dreamed it would pour."

spoor (sp*or*) a track or trail of someone or something being pursued

"The dog was trained to follow the **spoor** of wild animals."

stalch (st*aw*lch) in mining, an uncut piece of land surrounded by areas that have been worked

"Her lone house, standing alongside freeways, high-rises, office buildings, and giant parking lots, was like a **stalch**—an unmined oasis—that she intended to keep undisturbed for as long as she lived."

stellification (stelufiKĀshun) the process of making something, or someone, a star

"The **stellification** of that actress began with bit parts and ended with a show-stealing Oscar-winning performance."

stenotopic (stenuTOpik) able to tolerate only slight changes in temperature, humidity, and other environmental conditions

"When the temperature outside rose from 68 degrees to 90 degrees in only two hours, the **stenotopic** woman refused to go out."

stercoration (sterkuRĀshun) the act or process of spreading manure

"The antipornography group regarded distributors of pornography as engaged in **stercoration**."

stridor (STRĪder) sound of breathing, particularly in someone who has a chest cold

"Her labored **stridor** concerned her physician, who could easily tell that her breathing was obstructed."

struthionine (STRUtheunīn) like an ostrich

"Although the belief that ostriches bury their heads in the sand is without foundation, that **struthionine** image is a useful metaphor for people who ignore problems."

stull (stul) a support used in mines to prevent cave-ins

"Without sturdy **stulls**, mines would cave in much more often that they do."

For information about the *st* part of this word, see "instauration."

stygiophobia (STIJēōFŌbēu) fear of hell

"His **stygiophobia** was so strong that he couldn't even make one turn without using the turn signal, for fear that the illegal maneuver would condemn him to eternal damnation."

subarticulation (sub • *aw*rTIKy*u* • LĀshun) an interjection such as "aw," "uh-huh," "yick," or "whew," used to express surprise, agreement, or some other state of mind

"The teacher requested that her pupil say 'yes, ma'am,' and avoid 'uh-huh' and other casual **subarticulations**."

subaudition (sub • *aw*DISHun) the act of understanding, or ability to understand, something that is implied but not overtly expressed

"All it takes is a little bit of **subaudition** to get my drift (he probably doesn't even get what I mean by '**subaudition**'); do I have to spell it out for you?"

subboreal (subBORēul)   cold but not freezing

"It was forty degrees Fahrenheit, a stimulating, **subboreal** temperature."

subdititious (subdiTIshus)   involving a secret substitution

"When she substituted hamburger for steak, she thought her **subdititious** act would go unnoticed."

sup (sup)   a mouthful of liquid

"She was so thirsty that she enjoyed even the small **sup** of water."

supercalender (superCALunder)   to run through rollers in order to make smooth, emboss, or make thin

"The paper will not be usable until it has been **supercalendered**."

supererogate (supuRERugāt)   to do more than is required by duty or circumstances

"When she broke up the violent fight between the teenagers, she was **supererogating**."

supernaculum (superNAKyulum)   a drink that is good to the last drop

"The well-aged brandy was our **supernaculum**."

surd (serd)   quantity not expressible in rational numbers

"The square root of the number 3 is a **surd**."

syllabatim (siluBĀtim) syllable by syllable

"People who believe in the power of curses often contend that curses, to be effective, must be pronounced **syllabatim** and not slurred."

syncretism (sINKrutiz′m) an attempt (often illogical and leading to inconsistencies) to reconcile diverse or conflicting beliefs, especially in religion or philosophy

"She held that believing in animal rights *and* environmental ethics would result in a self-contradictory **syncretism** in which, for example, one would have both to oppose and to permit hunting for controlling animal populations."

synesthesia (sinisTHĒZyu) an effect on one of the senses produced by a stimulus to another, as a particular sight producing a sensation of a particular smell, or a sound seeming to have a certain color

"He regularly experienced **synesthesia**, as when he would smell bananas upon seeing yellow."

syngenesiotransplantation (sinjiNĒzēō • trans • plan • TĀshun) a graft of tissue between closely related individuals

"In a grand attempt at **syngenesiotransplantation**, the surgeon replaced the brother's heart with that of the sister."

syntagmatic (sintagMADik) determining the meaning of a word by considering it in the context of the sentence

"If we are to determine the meaning of a possibly ambiguous word, we need to look at the word **syntagmatically**."

T

tachytelic (takiTELik)   having a faster than normal rate of evolution for a specific group

"He wrote a science fiction novel in which the evolution of some members of a species was accelerated by a drug designed to produce **tachytelic** changes."

tack (tak)   to change course of a ship

"The President knew precisely when to **tack** the ship of state as the winds of public opinion changed."

talion (TALēun)   retaliation according to the principle of an eye for an eye

"She rejected the law of **talion** in favor of turning the other cheek."

tanling (TANling)   one whose skin is tanned by the sun

"We can usually distinguish people who are **tanlings** from those who go to tanning parlors."

tanquam (TANkwam)   one who has sufficient education to go to college

"Sadly, an alarming number of high school graduates are not even literates, much less **tanquams**."

taphephobia   (tafēFŌbeu)   fear of being buried alive

"We had always thought that her **taphephobia** was an entirely unreasonable fear—that is, until after she died, when we discovered that the inside of her casket lid had scratch marks from her fingernails."

"Tommy Warren, the used-book seller, joked that he had no **taphephobia**; in fact, he *expected* to be buried alive—under a ton of books fallen from one of his many rows of overflowing shelves."

tarantism   (TAruntiz′m)   an irresistible urge to dance

"A cynical writer from a conservative newspaper once ascribed **tarantism** to Michael Jackson because the writer disliked Jackson's energized dancing."

From the fifteenth to the seventeenth century a dancing malady or disease called tarantism existed in Europe and was common in Taranto, Italy, from which the sickness got its name. It was assumed that the disease was caused by the bite of the tarantula, a spider that also took its name from the Italian city. The tarantella, by the way, is a vivacious dance of southern Italy.

teratism   (TERutiz′m)   adoration of the monstrous

"We might regard the Aztec worship of their god as **teratism**, since it involved human sacrifice."

tergiversation (ter*jiver*SĀshun) abandoning a religion or cause

"In some religious traditions, people accused of **tergiversation** are more despised than infidels because the former, unlike the latter, are often regarded as not simply wrong but traitorously wrong."

tertius gaudens (TERtē*us* GOUdens) a third party who gloats over or profits from a dispute between two others

"A lawyer who has an interest in a conflict between two parties may well be a **tertius gaudens**."

Several Latin phrases containing the *gau* root have entered the English language, including *gaudet tentamine virtus* (virtue rejoices in trial), *gaudium certaminis* (the joy of battle), *gaudeamus igitur juvenes dum sumus* (let us therefore rejoice while we are young), and the Italian musical term *gaudioso* (exultant, gay).

Another Latin phrase with *terti* used in English is *tertium quid* (a third something; an intermediate, as between mind and matter).

thalassotherapy (thuLASuTHIRupē) an ocean cruise embarked upon as therapy

"She loves **thalassotherapy** but finds it hard to keep her weight down while tempted by all the food on the cruise."

thaumaturgy (THA*W*mu • *ter*jē) the working of miracles

"Because he was a thoroughgoing naturalist, he had little patience with claims of **thaumaturgy** and other magic."

thelyphthoric (thelifTHORik) corruptive to women

"The feminist insisted that pimps who wave lots of money in front of women are **thelyphthoric**."

theomachist (thēOMukist) one who opposes God

"The nineteenth-century American writer Robert Ingersoll was considered a **theomachist** because he used to dare God to strike him down."

tragomaschalia (trago · masKALyu), **hircismus** (herSIZmus) smelly armpits

"When we mailed him ten bottles of antiperspirant, he came to realize how offensive his **tragomaschalia** was to those around him."

The "hairy" part of this word is in the *trago* prefix. In fact, every common word that begins with *trag* in English has something to do with hair indirectly—very indirectly. That includes even "tragedy." The Greek word for "goat" is *tragos*, and goats are hairy creatures, hence the beard we call a goatee. Apparently, the ancient Greek tragedies were influenced by the Peloponnesian satyr play, which included a chorus of satyrs. The satyr was a grotesque mythological creature, essentially human but with the horns, ears, and legs of a goat.

translucent (transLUS'nt) light-admitting but not transparent

"Since the partition was **translucent** but not transparent, we knew there were two persons in the room, but we couldn't discern their identity."

transvection (transVEKshun) the supernatural conveyance of a witch through the air

"The witch claimed to need no airplanes but just her handy broom, by means of which she effected **transvection**."

The main roots of the word are *trans* (across) and *vect* (carry).

travail (truVĀL) childbirth pangs

"Some theologians argued against the use of anesthetic during childbirth on the grounds that the Bible in Genesis says that women shall experience **travail**."

trey (trā) three spots, as on a card or domino

"When she picked up the card, she saw the **trey** before she noticed the numeral three."

trig (trig) a stone, a brick, or some other obstacle placed under a wheel to prevent a conveyance from rolling

"We kept the wheelbarrow from rolling by placing a **trig** under the wheel."

trilemma (trīLEMu) a situation in which there are three unpleasant alternatives

"I am faced with the following **trilemma**: (1) I can blow the whistle on my company and probably lose my job; (2) I can do nothing and watch innocent customers be injured by our product; or (3) I can refuse to sign the form validating the product's safety and probably create an extremely tense work environment."

tutoyer (t*u*twuYĀ)   to address or treat familiarly a stranger

"It is impolite to **tutoyer** a high-ranking officer."

"**Tutoyer** the next person you pass on the sidewalk; she'll almost always appreciate it."

tutti (T*U*tē)   in music, a passage or movement in which all performers or instruments take part

"To most people, the sound of four persons all arguing simultaneously was awful, but to the controversial talk-show host, it was like pure **tutti**."

U

ubiquitous (y*u*BIKwutus)   being everywhere

"We considered the popular singer **ubiquitous** long before the publication of her revealing pictorial book, in which she was officially 'overexposed.'"

ucalegon (y*u*KALigon)   a neighbor whose house is on fire

"They called 911 to report a **ucalegon** badly in need of rescue by firefighters."

udney (UDnē)   an old friend whom you have outgrown; someone who loves you but does not understand you

"He became so intellectual and introspective that he regarded nearly everyone he knew as **udneys**."

udometer (y*u*DOMut*er*)   rain gauge

"We don't need a **udometer** to know that this rain is going to produce serious flooding in low-lying areas of the city."

ultima (ULtimu) the last syllable of a word

"We asked him to enunciate the **ultima** of every word ending with the suffix *-ing*, since he, like many others, tends to omit the *g* sound."

ultracrepidarianism (ultru • krepiDERēuniz′m) the habit of giving opinions and advice on matters outside one's knowledge

"His insinuating himself into our business was pure **ultracrepidarianism**."

ultrafidian (ultruFIDēun), **ultracredulous** extremely gullible

"The corrupt minister took advantage of his **ultrafidian** parishioners."

uzzard (UZud) third-generation bastard: a bastard by a bastard out of a bastard

"The politician condemned the welfare system for encouraging the production of **uzzards**."

V

vaccicide (VAKsisīd) killing of cows

"Were it not for Americans' acceptance of **vaccicide**, there would be no hamburgers."

vade mecum (vādē · MĒkum) a favorite book one carries everywhere

"Our editor's **vade mecum** is Fowler's *Modern English Usage*."

vagitus (vaJĪtus) cry of the newborn

"The carpenter told us that the creaky, settling noises we were hearing in our home were simply the **vagitus** of a newly built house."

valetudinarianism (valuT*U*DinERēuniz′m) preoccupied with one's illness

"She had little patience with her husband's **valetudinarianism**, since his complaints of illness prevented him from seeing his many blessings."

The *val* part of this word comes from the Indo-European root, *ual* (power, strength). The Latin word for "state of health" (one's strength) is *valetudo*. From the *ual* root English has "**val**iant" (remember, *u* and *v* are related), "**val**ence" (atomic strength), and "pre**vail**," as well as the names Arno**ld** (eagle strength), Gera**ld** (spear power), Haro**ld** (army leader), **Wal**ter (powerful warrior), Os**wald** (divine power), and Regina**ld** (powerful and mighty).

velivolant (vuLIVulunt) under full sail

"Although it was no fun hitching the sailboat up to the truck and hauling it to the marina, we knew that we'd quickly forget about those difficulties when we were **velivolant**."

velleity (vuLĒutē) a mere wish or desire unaccompanied by any attempt to attain it

"We knew that his desire to begin an exercise program was nothing more than a **velleity**, since he wasn't willing to begin such a program."

venatic (viNATik) living by hunting

"They needed large rifles for their **venatic** occupation."

voip (v*o*ip) food that is filling but tasteless

"We were so hungry that we went to our friend's house to gulp down some **voip**."

W

Wanderjahr (VONd*er* • yor)   a year of traveling before
settling down

  "Right after college she went to Europe for her
  Wanderjahr."

wanlasour (WONl'sur)   one who redirects a hunted animal toward the hunter

  "The **wanlasour** often rationalizes that he is not
  responsible for the killing but is only a dutiful middle-
  man who draws the victim into someone else's trap."

water-sick   irrigated to excess

  "With any more water, this land will become **water-
  sick** and suitable only for swimming or boating."

waveson (WĀVsun)   goods found floating in the sea
after a shipwreck

  "We know the ship was wrecked nearby, since all the
  waveson was found in this area."

wegotism (WĒgutiz'm) excessive use of "we," often sounding egotistical or conceited

"His **wegotism** made him sound more than a little snooty."

Weltschmerz (VELTshmerts) sadness over the evils of the world

"After reading Goethe's *The Sorrows of Young Werther*, many young Europeans were so overcome by **Weltschmerz** that they committed suicide."

wergild (WERgild) money paid to a slain man's kin

"The organization for the rights of crime victims argued for a **wergild** for slain people's families."

The *wer* part of this word is the same root that appears in the other popular *wer-* word, "**wer**ewolf." The *wer* means, quite simply, "man," hence "man-wolf." A variant of this root gives us "**vir**ile," "**vir**tue," and, perhaps most interestingly, "**wor**ld," which originates from an Old English word meaning, literally, "life, or "age" (*old*) "of man" (*weor*), thus *weorold*—world.

X

xenogenesis (zenuJENusis) the supposed procreation of offspring who are completely different biologically from the parents, as in spontaneous generation

"I don't believe that wolves can give birth to human beings or that there exists any other form of **xenogenesis**."

The *xeno* root comes from Greek *xenos*, meaning "stranger." It has given us "**xen**ophobia" (fear or hatred of foreigners), "**xen**ophilia" (love of strangers or foreigners), "**xen**ogogue" (a leader of strangers, hence a tour guide), and "pyro**xene**" (literally, a stranger to fire—that is, a mineral that does not occur in igneous rock).

xenoglossia (zenuGLAWSēu) the ability to speak a foreign language without ever having consciously learned it

"She doubts whether there has ever been a scientifically documented case of **xenoglossia** and holds that the alleged instances are either fraudulent cases concocted by charlatans or cases in which people are speaking gibberish."

xylophilous   (zīLOFulus)   living in or on wood

"I want those termites out of my home; the **xylophilous** creatures aren't even paying rent."

The *xyl* root in this word is related to the *syl* in "**syl**van" (of the forest, from which wood comes), the *sal* in "**sal**ubrious" (healthful, which the forest can be), and ultimately "**salt**." (To see how "**salt**" produced "**syl**van" and several other words, see "**hal**obios.")

Y

yaffling   (YAFling)   eating greedily and noisily

"His **yaffling** was disturbing the quiet, well-mannered patrons at the cafeteria."

yamnoy   (YAMn*oi*)   an object so bulky, slippery, or cumbersome that it is difficult to carry

"There's no way he'll even consider carrying this **yamnoy** unless he has the help of several strong workers."

yaw   (y*aw*)   to deviate from one's course

"Do not let rejections cause you to **yaw**; you must stick to your dreams and goals and not veer from your course."

"Quite unexpectedly, the ship **yawed** to starboard."

Z

Zeigarnik (zĭGAWRnik) **effect** the tendency to remember unfinished business and to forget finished business

> "I procrastinate so much that, because of the **Zeigarnik effect**, there's practically nothing that I don't remember."

The term is derived from Bluma Zeigarnik, a twentieth-century German psychologist. In one of Zeigarnik's experiments, the psychologist gave a group of subjects twenty tasks, ten of which they were allowed to complete. As each of the other ten tasks was removed, the subjects were told, "That is enough now; turn to this other task." At the end the subjects were asked to list as many tasks as they could recall. Since the subjects recalled more of the unfinished tasks than the finished ones, the tendency to remember unfinished business is called the Zeigarnik effect.

ThesauroIndex

ABILITY/INABILITY (see also KNOWLEDGE/
    STUPIDITY, PAIN, PROBLEMS, STRATEGY)
  acalculia, alexia, aprosexia, baragnosis, chimera, dub/
  palooka, hwyl, illachrymable, kakistocracy, law of exer-
  cise, malinger, numerate, one-trial learning
ABNORMALITY   see GROWTH
ABSENCE   see CONNECTION/GAP/LOSS
ABSTRACT/CONCRETE (see also DECEPTION,
    STONES, THINGS/REALITY)
  concretize, reify
ABSURDITY   see REASON
ACCIDENTS   see WRECKS
ACCUSATION   see ARGUMENT
ADDICTION   see WILLPOWER
ADMIRATION   see LOVE/HATE
ADORATION   see LOVE/HATE
ADULTERY   see MARRIAGE
ADVERTISING (see also MONEY, SPEAKING,
    THINGS/REALITY, WRITING)
  admass
ADVICE   see QUESTION/ANSWER
AFFECTATION   see DECEPTION
AGE (see also CHILDREN, GROWTH/DEFORMITY,
    NUMBERS, TIME)
  agerasia, caducity, consensus gentium fallacy, craquelure,

doyen, gerascophobia, gerontocracy, juvenescent, metrona, paedogenetic, poliosis, pornogenarian)

AGGRESSION   see FIGHTING

AIR   (see also BREATHING, COVERING [AS IN CLOUDS], SMELL, SMOKING, STARS, SUN)
apteryx, emunction, konimeter, miasma, transvection

ALCOHOL   (see also DROPS/DROPPING/DRIPPING, LIQUID, MEDICINE, WATER, WILLPOWER)
gambrinous, potvaliant

ALONE   see CROWDS

ANGER   see LOVE/HATE

ANIMALS   (see also CHILDREN, FOOD, GROWTH/ DEFORMITY, HOME, HUNTING, INSECTS, MEN/WOMEN, NATURE, WASTE)
ailurophile, ailurophobe, anthropopithecus, apteryx, banderilla, biophillism, deadset, disgorger, formicide, gallinicide, halobios, hippomaniac, latrability, onomatopoeic, paedogenetic, pollard, snuffle, vaccicide

ANSWERS   see QUESTION/ANSWER

ANTS   see INSECTS

ANXIETIES   see FEARS

APOLOGY   see CONFESSION/FORGIVENESS/ REMORSE

APPLAUSE   (see also PRAISE, SHOWS)
claqueur

APPRECIATION   see PRAISE

APPROPRIATE   see GOOD

APPROVAL   see PRAISE

ARGUMENT   (see also BELIEF[S], DECEPTION, EARTHQUAKES, FIGHTING, FRIENDS/ STRANGERS, KNOWLEDGE/STUPIDITY, LOVE/ HATE, OPPOSITENESS, PUNISHMENT, QUESTION/ANSWER, REASON/ILLOGICALITY, SPEAKING, WARNING[S]/THREAT[S], WORDS) admass, apaetesis, asphalia, asteism, catarolysis, charientism, consensus gentium fallacy, epitrope, expeditio, fallacy of the beard, gambler's fallacy, gravamen, modus vivendi, parley, pilpul, prolepsis, Quinapalus, tertius gaudens

ARITHMETIC   see MATH

ARMS   see BODY

ART   (see also DOLLS, PAINTINGS)
  mataeotechny

ASTROLOGY   see STARS

ATMOSPHERE   see AIR

ATTACK   see FIGHTING

ATTENTION   see VISION or INDIFFERENCE/
      OVERCONCERN

AUDIENCE   (see also SHOWS, SOUND, VISION)
  claqueur, quonking

AUTOMOBILES   see TRAVEL

BABIES   see CREATIVITY/NEWNESS or CHILDREN

BAD   see GOOD/BAD

BALANCING   (see also DIFFERENTNESS/CHANGE/
      SAMENESS)
  equilibritist/schoenabatist

BARKING   see ANIMALS

BASICS   see KNOWLEDGE/STUPIDITY or FIRST/
      LAST

BASTARD   (see also CHILDREN)
  uzzard

BEAUTY   (see also BODY, CHARACTER, COVERING,
      MAKEUP, SEX, VISION)
  Adonis, calligraphy, dyscalligynia, kaleidogyn, prosopolepsy

BED   see SLEEP

BEGINNINGS   see FIRST

BEHAVIOR   see GOOD

BELIEF(S) (see also DECEPTION, KNOWLEDGE/
    STUPIDITY, REASON/ILLOGICALITY, RELI-
    GION, RULE-MAKERS/RULE-FOLLOWERS,
    STRICTNESS, SUPERNATURAL, THOUGHT)
antinomian, anacoenosis, biophillism, cleocentric, con-
sensus gentium fallacy, eidolism, equalitarian, euhemer-
ism, girouettism, grandgousier, henotheism, iatrapistia,
iconoclast, latitudinarian, mumpsimus, solipsism, syncre-
tism, ultracrepidarianism, ultrafidian/ultracredulous
BELLS   see SOUND
BIAS   see EQUALITY/FAIRNESS/BIAS
BIBLE   see RELIGION
BIG   see LARGENESS/SMALLNESS
BIRTH   see CREATIVITY/NEWNESS or CHILDREN
BITING   see MOUTH
BLEMISHES   see PIMPLES
BLINDNESS   see VISION
BLOOD   (see also HEART, CONNECTION/GAP/LOSS,
    BODY)
aceldama, parabiosis, phagocytose
BLOWING   see AIR
BODY   (see also BEAUTY, COVERING [AS IN
    CLOTHING], BONES, FEELING[S], FEET,
    HAIRS/HAIR-THIN, HANDS, HEAD, HEART,
    ILLNESS/HEALTHINESS, MAKEUP, MOUTH,
    NOSE, PAIN, PIMPLES, SEX, SKIN, THROAT,
    TISSUES, WOUNDS)
acromegalic, disembosom, kakidrosis, kermes,
marasmic/marantic, oxter, resurrectionist, resupination,
tragomaschalia
BONES   (see also BODY, SHELLS, STONES)
snuffle
BOOKS   see WORDS
BOREDOM   see TIREDNESS

BORROWING   see GIVING/TAKING
BOSS   see LEADERS/LEADERSHIP
BOWL   see PLATES AND PANS
BRANCHES   see CONNECTION/GAP/LOSS
BREAKING   see CUTTING
BREATHING   (see also AIR, NOSE)
  fnast/fnese, stridor
BRICKS   see STONES
BRIGHTNESS   see LIGHT/DARK
BRISTLES   see HAIRS/HAIRTHIN
BROKEN   see CONNECTION/GAP/LOSS
BROTHERS   see FAMILY
BUGS   see INSECTS
BUILDINGS   (see also CITY, HOME, SPACES,
      THINGS/REALITY)
  belvedere
BULKY   see CARRYING
BUREAUCRATS   see WORK
BURIAL   see DEATH
BURNING   see FIRE
BUYING   see MONEY
CALM   see PEACE
CAPABILITY   see ABILITY/INABILITY
CAPTURED/CAPTURING   (see also HUNTING,
      OPEN/CLOSE)
  backberend
CARE   see LOVE
CARELESSNESS   see INDIFFERENCE/
      OVERCONCERN
CARRYING   (see also DIRECTIONS, DROPS/
      DROPPING/DRIPPING, FEELING[S], HANDS,
      TRAVEL, WEIGHT)
  fomites, yamnoy
CATS   see ANIMALS

CAUSE/EFFECT   (see also CREATIVITY/NEWNESS,
        EVENTS, KNOWLEDGE/STUPIDITY, PROB-
        LEMS, REASON/ILLOGICALITY, STRATEGY)
   iatrogenic, kedogenous, naufragous, photopathy, ptocho-
   gony, synesthesia
CELEBRATION   see EVENTS
CELLS   see NATURE
CERTAINTY   see GUARANTEES/CERTAINTY
CHANGE   see LUCK
CHANGE   see DIFFERENTNESS
CHAOS   see GOOD
CHARACTER   (see also FEELINGS, BEAUTY,
        LOVE/HATE, MEN/WOMEN, NATURE)
   cowcat, eidolon, ethos, hamartia, mucker pose, pheno-
   type, prosopography, udney
CHEATING   see DECEPTION
CHESS   see PLAYING
CHEWING   see FOOD
CHILDREN   (see also ANIMALS, BASTARD,
        CREATIVITY/NEWNESS, DOLLS, FAMILY,
        GROWTH/DEFORMITY, MARRIAGE, MEN/
        WOMEN, NATURE, SEX)
   agenocratia, catadromous, imago, mammothrept,
   marasmic/marantic, natalitious, nullipara, paedogenetic,
   travail, uzzard, vagitus, xenogenesis
CHIMES   see SOUND
CHOICES   see STRATEGY
CHOOSING   see STRATEGY
CHRISTIANITY   see RELIGION
CIGARETTES   see SMOKING
CIRCLE   see DIRECTION
CIRCULATION   see HEART
CITY   (see also BUILDINGS, COUNTRY, GOVERN-
        MENT, SPACES, WORLD/EVERYTHING)
   hippodamist

CLARITY   see VISION
CLEANING   see DIRT
CLIMBING   see SUCCESS/FAILURE or WALKING or
     MOUNTAINS
CLOSED   see OPEN/CLOSE
CLOSENESS   see CONNECTION/GAP/LOSS
CLOTHING   see COVERING
CLOUDS   see COVERING
COINS   see MONEY
COLD/HOT   (see also FIRE, LIGHT/DARK, MATCH-
     BOXES, SUN)
  adiathermic, subboreal
COLLECTION/COLLECTING   (see also CARRYING,
     HUNTING, WILLPOWER/COMPULSION/
     CONTROL, VISION)
  conchology, congeries, cumyxaphily, discophily, ph-
  langonologist
COLORS   (see also FEELING[S], LIGHT/DARK,
     VISION)
  achromatopsia/daltonism, albescent, chiaroscuro, isoch-
  romous, poliosis
COMMUNICATION   see WORDS or THOUGHT
COMPETITION   see PLAYING
COMPLAINT   see ARGUMENT
COMPLIMENTS   see PRAISE
COMPULSION   see WILLPOWER/COMPULSION/
     CONTROL
COMPUTATION   see MATH
CONCEIT   see IMPORTANCE/UNIMPORTANCE
CONCENTRATION   see THOUGHT
CONCERN   see INDIFFERENCE/OVERCONCERN
CONCLUSIONS   see FIRST/LAST or REASON/
     ILLOGICALITY
CONCRETE   see ABSTRACT

CONFESSION/FORGIVENESS/REMORSE (see also
    GOOD/BAD, HAPPINESS/UNHAPPINESS,
    PROMISE, RELIGION, RESIGNATION/GIVING
    UP)
  antapology
CONFIDENTIAL see SECRECY/SECRETS/
    SURPRISING
CONFUSION see KNOWLEDGE/STUPIDITY
CONGRATULATIONS see PRAISE
CONNECTION/GAP/LOSS (see also BLOOD [AS IN
    CIRCULATION], DEATH, FAMILY, FIRST/
    LAST, GOOD/BAD [AS IN WELL MATCHED],
    MARRIAGE, MEMORY, TIME)
  anthropopithecus, antisyzygy, asymptotically, concinnity,
  confabulation, craquelure, inosculate, Kallikak, parabio-
  sis, retiary, revenant, seriatim, stipple, syngenesiotrans-
  plantation, syntagmatic
CONTAINERS see COVERING
CONTAMINATION see POISON
CONTROL see WILLPOWER/COMPULSION/
    CONTROL
CONTROLLING see OPEN/CLOSE
CONVERSATION see SPEAKING
COOKING see FOOD
COUNTRY (see also CITY, GOVERNMENT, NATURE,
    SPACES, WORLD/EVERYTHING)
  anachorism, Balkanize, Lebensraum, rusticate
COURAGE (see also FEARS, INDIFFERENCE/
    OVERCONCERN)
  oriflamme, potvaliant
COURT see LAW
COVERING (see also AIR [AS IN CLOUDS], DECEP-
    TION, HAPPINESS/UNHAPPINESS [AS IN
    CLOUDS OF GLOOM], KNOWLEDGE/

STUPIDITY, MAKEUP, OPEN/CLOSE,
SECRECY/SECRETS/SURPRISE, SHADOW,
SHELLS, SMOKING)

beauism, deaconing, deciduous, dishabille, dishabillophobia, galericulate, immerd, instar, latebricole, misapodysis, nelipot, nepheligenous, nephometer, paletoted,
scotoma, stercoration, struthionine, subaudition, translucent

CRACK   see CONNECTION/GAP/LOSS

CRAWING   (see also TRAVEL, WALKING)

formication

CRAYONS   (see also PICTURES, WRITING,
KNOWLEDGE/STUPIDITY)

calcographer

CREATIVITY/NEWNESS   (see also ART, CAUSE/
EFFECT, CHILDREN [AS IN BIRTH], FIRST/
LAST, GROWTH/DEFORMITY, WORK, WRIT-
ING)

benedict, calathus, misocainia, neologism, orogeny, paroemiology, parturient, parvenu, poncif

CRIME   (see also DECEPTION, FIGHTING,
GIVING/TAKING, LAW, WAR)

blabagogy, fagin, scofflaw

CROWDS   (see also AUDIENCE, FRIENDS/
STRANGERS, ONE)

admass, bandwagon fallacy, bellwether, consensus gentium fallacy, gapeseed, girouettism, mumpsimus

CRYING   (see also CONFESSION/FORGIVENESS/
REMORSE, HAPPINESS/UNHAPPINESS,
LIQUID, VISION, WATER)

illachrymable, vagitus

CURVING   see TURNING

CUTTING   (see also FIGHTING, HAIRS/HAIR-THIN,
MEDICINE, NEEDLES/PINS, OPEN/CLOSE,

POKING/PRICKING . . . , SCRATCHING/
TICKLING)

acersecomic, Balkanize, debridement, grangerize, pone, stalch

DANCING (see also WALKING)

tarantism

DARK see LIGHT/DARK

DARTS see POKING/PRICKING . . .

DATING see LOVE/HATE

DAY see TIME

DEADLINE see TIME

DEATH (see also CONNECTION/GAP/LOSS, FIGHT-
ING, FIRST/LAST, HELL, HUNTING, WAR,
WASTE)

amicicide, anabiosis, anacampserote, banshee, civil death, debridement, doppelgänger, formicide, gallinicide, kachina, lugubrious, mactation, moirologist, Moloch, necromimesis, preagonal, taphephobia, vaccicide, wergild

DEBT (see also GAMBLING, GIVING/TAKING,
GUARANTEES/CERTAINTY, MONEY)

dun

DECEPTION (see also ARGUMENT, BELIEFS, COV-
ERING, CRIME, EQUALITY/FAIRNESS/
BIAS, GIVING/TAKING, GROWTH/DEFORMITY,
PROMISE, REASON/ILLOGICALITY, SECRECY/
SECRETS/SURPRISE, SHADOW, VISION, YARN
[AS IN TALL TALE])

acouasm, banderilla, charientism, confabulation, deaconing, dereism, doppelgänger, foma, imago, malinger, man-
aged text, miasma, mucker pose, necromimesis, oneirataxia, penelopize, roorback

DECISIONS see STRATEGY

DECREASE see NUMBERS

DEEDS   see GOOD/BAD

DEEPNESS   see LENGTH/DEPTH

DEFEATING   see SUCCESS/FAILURE

DEFECTS   see GROWTH/DEFORMITY

DEFENSE   see WAR or ARGUMENT

DEFORMITY   see GROWTH/DEFORMITY

DEGREE   see LENGTH/DEPTH

DELAYING   see TIME

DELUSIONS   see DECEPTION

DEPENDENCE/INDEPENDENCE   (see also GIVING/
     TAKING, LEADERS/LEADERSHIP, LOVE/HATE,
     MARRIAGE, ONE)
  anaclitic, aseity

DEPRESSION   see HAPPINESS/UNHAPPINESS

DEPTH   see LENGTH/DEPTH

DESIRES   see WANT

DESTROYING   see FIGHTING

DESTRUCTION   see DEATH

DEVELOPMENT   see GROWTH/DEFORMITY

DIETING   see FOOD

DIFFERENTNESS/CHANGE/SAMENESS   (see also
     ARGUMENT, BALANCING, EQUALITY/
     FAIRNESS/BIAS, GROWTH/DEFORMITY, OP-
     POSITENESS, SPEED, STRATEGY, TURNING)
  anachorism, asonia, bradytelic, deus ex machina, emulous, equiponderate, gongoozler, instar, isochromous, misocainia, oneirataxia, stenotopic, syncretism, tachytelic,
  tack, trilemma, yaw

DIFFICULTY   see ABILITY/INABILITY

DIMENSIONS   see LENGTH/DEPTH or LARGENESS/
     SMALLNESS

DINNER   see FOOD

DIRECTION   (see also CARRYING, LEADERS/
     LEADERSHIP, POKING/PRICKING . . . [AS IN

POINTING], SPEED, STARS, SUCCESS/
FAILURE [AS IN MOVING UPWARD],
THOUGHT, THROWING, TRAVEL, TURNING)

catadromous, decubitus, dextrovert, orthodromics, photopathy, pone, porrect, sigmoidal, signpost writing, tack,
velivolant, wanlasour

DIRT/CLEANING   (see also GOOD/BAD, LAND, POI-
SON, SEX, WASTE)

despumate, konimeter, molysmophobia/mysophobia

DISAGREEMENT   see ARGUMENT

DISAPPEARANCE   see VISION

DISCHARGE   see THROWING

DISCOMFORT   see PAIN

DISCUSSION   see ARGUMENT

DISEASE   see ILLNESS

DISGUST   see LOVE/HATE

DISLIKE   see LOVE/HATE

DISORGANIZED   see GOOD/BAD

DISPLAYING   see VISION

DISPUTE   see ARGUMENT

DISTANCE   see LENGTH/DEPTH

DISTORTION   see DECEPTION

DIVIDING   see CUTTING or TWO

DIVINE   see RELIGION

DIVORCED   see MARRIAGE

DOCTORS   see MEDICINE

DOCTRINE   see BELIEF(S)

DOGMA   see BELIEF(S)

DOGS   see ANIMALS

DOLLARS   see MONEY

DOLLS   (see also CHILDREN)

kachina, phlangonologist

DOTS   see SPOTS

DOUBLE   see TWO

DOUBT   see PROCRASTINATION
DRAMA   (see also HAPPINESS/UNHAPPINESS,
      SHOWS)
  denouement
DREAMS   see SLEEP
DRESSING   see COVERING
DRINKING   see LIQUID
DRIVING   see TRAVEL
DROPS/DROPPING/DRIPPING   (see also CARRYING,
      NUMBERS, SUCCESS/FAILURE)
  deciduous, enew, supernaculum
DUNG   see WASTE
DUPLICATION   see REPETITION/DUPLICATION
DURABILITY   see STRENGTH/WEAKNESS
DUST   see DIRT/CLEANING
DUTY   see WORK
EARS   see SOUND
EARTH   (see also HOME, LAND, NATURE, WORLD)
  ageotropic
EARTHQUAKES   (see also ARGUMENT, FIGHTING,
      LAND)
  kratogen
EASINESS   see ABILITY/INABILITY
EATING   see FOOD
EFFECT   see CAUSE/EFFECT
EFFORT   see WORK
EGOTISM   see IMPORTANCE/UNIMPORTANCE
ELDERLY   see AGE
ELECTION   see LEADERS/LEADERSHIP
ELEMENTS   see NATURE
EMBARRASSMENT   see CONFESSION/
      FORGIVENESS/REMORSE
EMBLEMS   see SYMBOLS
EMOTIONS   see FEELING(S)

EMPLOY   see WORK

EMPTY   see CONNECTION/GAP/LOSS

ENCLOSURE   see COVERING

END   see FIRST/LAST

ENEMY   see FIGHTING

ENTERTAINMENT   see SHOWS

ENTRANCE   see OPEN/CLOSE

ENVIRONMENT   see WORLD/EVERYTHING

EQUALITY/FAIRNESS/BIAS   (see also DECEPTION,
   DIFFERENTNESS/CHANGE/SAMENESS,
   GIVING/TAKING, GOOD/BAD, LAW, LOVE/
   HATE, REASON/ILLOGICALITY)

  biophillism, civil death, eisegesis, equalitarian, isocracy,
  isonomy, mumpsimus, prosopolepsy

EQUALNESS (IN GENERAL)   see
   DIFFERENTNESS/CHANGE/SAMENESS

ERASABLE   see OPEN/CLOSE

EROSION   see POKING/PRICKING

ERROR   see GOOD/BAD or KNOWLEDGE/
   STUPIDITY

ESCAPE   see OPEN/CLOSE

ETHNICITY   see SKIN or COLORS

EVENNESS   see EQUALITY/FAIRNESS/BIAS or
   FLATNESS

EVENTS   (see also CAUSE/EFFECT, NEWS, SHOWS,
   TIME)

  deus ex machina, gapeseed, instant book / extra / quickie,
  law of recency, nonce word

EVERYTHING   see WORLD/EVERYTHING

EVIDENCE   see INFORMATION

EVIL   see GOOD/BAD

EVOLUTION   see DIFFERENTNESS/CHANGE/
   SAMENESS

EXCITEMENT   see HAPPINESS/UNHAPPINESS

EXCREMENT   see WASTE
EXCUSE   see REASON/ILLOGICALITY
EXISTENCE   see THINGS/REALITY
EXIT   see OPEN/CLOSE
EXPLOSION   see THROWING
EYES   see VISION
FACTS   see INFORMATION
FAILURE   see SUCCESS/FAILURE
FAIRNESS   see EQUALITY/FAIRNESS/BIAS
FAITH   see BELIEF(S)
FAITHFULNESS   see BELIEF(S)
FALLACIES   see ARGUMENT
FALLING   see SUCCESS/FAILURE or DROPS/
      DROPPING/DRIPPING
FALSITY   see DECEPTION
FAME   see SUCCESS/FAILURE
FAMILIARITY   see FRIENDS/STRANGERS
FAMILY   (see also ANIMALS, CHILDREN, GROWTH/
      DEFORMITY, HOME, MARRIAGE, MEN/
      WOMEN, SEX)
   anaclitic, heredipety, imago, kachina, Kallikak, metrona,
   pentheraphobia, phenotype, soceraphobia, wergild
FANTASY   see DECEPTION
FARMING   see PLANTS or ANIMALS
FASCINATION   see LOVE/HATE
FASTNESS   see SPEED
FAT   (see also LARGENESS/SMALLNESS)
   lipolysis
FATHER   see MEN/WOMEN
FAVORITISM   see EQUALITY/FAIRNESS/BIAS
FEARS   (see also HAPPINESS/UNHAPPINESS,
      INDIFFERENCE/OVERCONCERN)
   aichmophobia, amblysia, anuptaphobia, ballistophobia,
   catagelophobia, clinophobia, dishabillophobia, gerasco-

phobia, hamartophobia, hodophobia, horripilation, hypengyophobia, iatrophobia, ictal emotions, kakorrhaphiophobia, kedogenous, molysmophobia/mysophobia, nosocomephobia, onomatophobia, paralipophobia, pentheraphobia, psellismophobia, scotophobia, stygiophobia, taphephobia

FEELING(S) (see also BODY, CHARACTER [AS IN EMOTIONAL MAKEUP], COLORS, CREATIVITY/NEWNESS, FLAVOR, HANDS, HAPPINESS/UNHAPPINESS, LOVE/HATE, MOUTH, NOSE, PAIN, SEX, SMELL, SOUND, TASTE, THOUGHT, VISION)

admanuensis, anhedonia, bletonism, formication, hwyl, ictal emotions, Rorschach test, subarticulation, synesthesia

FEET (see also RUNNING, STANDING, TRAVEL, WALKING)

acronyx, discalceate, hallux, nelipot, podobromhidrosis

FEMALES see MEN

FENCES see OPEN

FIGHTING (see also ARGUMENT, CRIME, CUTTING, DEATH, EARTHQUAKES, HAMMER, HUNTING, LOVE/HATE, OPPOSITENESS, POKING/ PRICKING . . . , PUNISHMENT, SCRATCHING/ TICKLING, STRENGTH/WEAKNESS, THROWING, WAR)

aceldama, Balkanize, ballistophobia, banderilla, forfoughten, hieromachy, holmgang, iconoclast, naumachy, oriflamme, phagocytose, sockdolager, talion, theomachist

FINGERS see HANDS

FIRE (see also COLD/HOT, LIGHT/DARK, SMOKING, SUN)

firebreak, ucalegon

FIRST/LAST (see also CAUSE/EFFECT, CHILDREN,

CONNECTION/GAP/LOSS, CREATIVITY/
NEWNESS, DEATH, INCOMPLETENESS,
LEADERS/LEADERSHIP, MOUTH, NUMBERS,
ONE, SUCCESS/FAILURE, TIME)

aporia, catagraph, charette, cliack, denouement, exordium, fallacy of the beard, lysis, one-trial learning, penultima, penultimate, preantepenultimate, prolegomena, qualtagh, Sherman statement, ultima

FISH   see ANIMALS

FLAGS   see SYMBOLS

FLATNESS   (see also PLATES AND PANS,
      SCRATCHING/TICKLING [AS IN ERODING])

peneplain/peneplane, porrect, supercalender

FLATTERY   (see also DECEPTION, FRIENDS/
      STRANGERS, LOVE/HATE)

gixlety

FLAVOR   (see also COLORS, FEELING[S], FOOD,
      MOUTH, TASTE)

phonaesthesia

FLOWERS   see PLANTS

FLYING   see AIR

FOOD (see also ANIMALS, GRAIN, GROWTH/
      DEFORMITY, HUNTING, MOUTH, NATURE,
      OPEN/CLOSE [AS IN DEVOURING], PLANTS,
      PLATES AND PANS, TASTE, WASTE, WATER)

acetarious, bantingism, bouffage, cleptobiosis/lestobiosis, critouns, deaconing, Fletcherize, grandgousier, logophagist, lubber-wort, omnivorous, opsomania, padrone, psomophagy, rasorial, smell-feast, supernaculum, voip, yaffling

FOREST   see PLANTS

FOREVER   see TIME

FORGETTING   see MEMORY

FORGIVING   see CONFESSION/FORGIVENESS/
        REMORSE
FREEDOM   see WILLPOWER/COMPULSION/
        CONTROL
FREEZING   see COLD/HOT
FRIENDS/STRANGERS (see also CROWDS,
        DIFFERENTNESS/CHANGE, GIVING/TAKING,
        LOVE/HATE, MEN/WOMEN, NICENESS)
  amicicide, disembosom, gowyop, oxter, phatic, tutoyer,
  udney
FRONT   see DIRECTION
FRUIT   see PLANTS
FUNDAMENTALS   see KNOWLEDGE/STUPIDITY or
        FIRST/LAST
FUNNY   see LAUGHTER
GAMBLING   (see also DEBT, GIVING/TAKING,
        GUARANTEES/CERTAINTY, MONEY)
  equilibritist/schoenabatist, gambler's fallacy, martingale
GAMES   see PLAYING
GAP   see CONNECTION
GAWKING   see VISION
GENES   see FAMILY
GENITALS   see BODY
GHOSTS   see SUPERNATURAL
GIVING/TAKING   (see also CRIME, DEBT, DECEP-
        TION, EQUALITY/FAIRNESS/BIAS, FIGHTING,
        LOVE/HATE, MONEY, OPEN/CLOSE, PRAISE,
        WASTE)
  backberend, batten, cleptobiosis/lestobiosis, kleptocracy,
  Moloch, pismirism, resurrectionist
GIVING UP   see RESIGNATION/GIVING UP
GOALS   see WANT
GOD   see RELIGION
GOLD   see MONEY

GOOD/BAD   (see also BEAUTY, CHARACTER,
     CONFESSION/FORGIVENESS/REMORSE,
     DIFFERENTNESS/CHANGE/SAMENESS, DIRT/
     CLEANING, EQUALITY/FAIRNESS/BIAS,
     FEELING[S], FIGHTING, FRIENDS/
     STRANGERS, GIVING/TAKING, GROWTH/
     DEFORMITY, HAPPINESS/UNHAPPINESS,
     HEART, ILLNESS/HEALTHINESS, KNOW-
     LEDGE/STUPIDITY, LAUGHTER, LENGTH/
     DEPTH [AS IN LOWNESS/EVIL], LOVE/HATE,
     NICENESS, PAIN, POISON, RELIGION, SLEEP
     [AS IN NIGHTMARES], SMELL [AS IN
     STENCH]
   agathokakological, amblysia, anachorism, anomie, apotropaic, beauism, belvedere, cacophonophilist, concinnity, daub, ersatz, exemplar, fastigium, hamartia,
   hamartophobia, hesternopathia, heterogamosis, imago,
   insilium, instauration, kakistocracy, Kallikak, matutolypea, miasma, *mot propre*, nomogamosis, obelize/athetize,
   obsidium, orthodromics, pornogenarian, supererogate,
   teratism, thaumaturgy, thelyphthoric
GOSSIP   see SPEAKING
GOVERNMENT   (see also CITY, COUNTRY, CRIME,
     LAW, LEADERS/LEADERSHIP, RULE-MAKERS/
     RULE-FOLLOWERS)
   anomie, gerontocracy, hagiarchy, isocracy, kakistocracy,
   kleptocracy, plutocracy, ptochocracy
GRAIN   (see also GROWTH, PLANTS)
   cliack
GRAMMAR   see WORDS
GRANDMOTHER   see FAMILY
GRATITUDE   see PRAISE
GRAVES   see DEATH
GREATNESS   see LARGENESS

GREED   see GIVING

GROWTH/DEFORMITY   (see also AGE, ANIMALS,
    BODY, CHILDREN, CREATIVITY/NEWNESS,
    DIFFERENTNESS/CHANGE/SAMENESS,
    FOOD, GOOD/BAD, HOME, INSECTS,
    KNOWLEDGE/STUPIDITY, MEN/WOMEN,
    PLANTS, STRATEGY, TIME, TURNING,
    WRINKLES)

  acromegalic, acronyx, adnascent, batten, bradyauxesis,
  heliotropic, jarovize, latebricole, Lebensraum, lotic, photobiotic, poliosis, saprophilous, serotinous, udney, venatic

GUARANTEES/CERTAINTY   (see also GAMBLING,
    KNOWLEDGE/STUPIDITY)

  asphalia, logophagist

GULLIBILITY   see BELIEF(S)

HABIT   see WILLPOWER/COMPULSION/CONTROL

HAIRS/HAIR-THIN   (see also CONNECTION/GAP/
    LOSS, CUTTING, LARGENESS/SMALLNESS,
    LENGTH/DEPTH, NEEDLES/PINS, RODS, YARN)

  acersecomic, albescent, equilibritist/schoenabatist, hirci,
  pilpul, poliosis

HAMMER   (see also FIGHTING)

  patellar reflex

HANDS   (see also BODY, CARRYING, FEELING[S],
    POKING/PRICKLING, SCRATCHING/
    TICKLING)

  akimbo, calligraphy, gowpen, lirp, phaneromania, pugil

HAPPINESS/UNHAPPINESS   (see also CONFESSION/
    FORGIVENESS/REMORSE, COVERING [AS IN
    CLOUDS OF GLOOM], CRYING, FEARS, FEEL-
    ING[S], GOOD/BAD, ILLNESS/HEALTHINESS,
    LOVE/HATE, PAIN, PEACE, RAIN [AS IN MIS-

FORTUNE], SCRATCHING/TICKLING, SEX,
WAR)

anhedonia, bouffage, cagamosis, confelicity, eudaemonia,
ictal emotions, longanimity, lugubrious, malneirophrenia,
matutolypea, nympholepsy, trilemma, Weltschmerz

HARDNESS   see STRENGTH/WEAKNESS

HARMFUL   see GOOD/BAD

HATE   see LOVE/HATE

HATS   see COVERING

HEAD   (see also THOUGHT)

acouasm, struthionine

HEALTH   see ILLNESS/HEALTHINESS

HEARING   see SOUND

HEART   (see also BLOOD, CONNECTION/GAP/LOSS,
BODY, LOVE/HATE)

bradycardia

HEAT   see COLD/HOT or LIGHT/DARK or SUN

HEAVINESS   see WEIGHT

HEIGHT   see LENGTH/DEPTH

HELL   (see also PAIN, PUNISHMENT, RELIGION)

hadeharia, stygiophobia

HESITATION   see SPEED

HIDING   see COVERING

HIGHNESS   see LENGTH/DEPTH

HISTORY   see TIME

HITTING   see FIGHTING

HOLES   see SPACES

HOLINESS   see RELIGION

HOLLOW   see CONNECTION/GAP/LOSS

HOME   (see also BUILDINGS, FAMILY, GROWTH/
DEFORMITY, NATURE)

circumforaneous, cryptoscopophilia, knickknackatory, latebricole, padrone, qualtagh, rackrent, rusticate, ucalegon, Wanderjahr, xylophilous

HONESTY   see BELIEF(S)
HOOK   (see also CUTTING, HUNTING, TURNING)
  disgorger
HOPES   see WANT
HOSPITALS   see MEDICINE
HOT   see COLD/HOT
HOUSE   see HOME
HUMANS   see MEN/WOMEN
HUMILIATION   see CONFESSION/FORGIVENESS/
      REMORSE
HUMOR   see LAUGHTER
HUNTING   (see also ANIMALS, CAPTURED/
      CAPTURING, DEATH, DECEPTION, DIREC-
      TION, FOOD, MINING, TRAVEL, VISION,
      WANT)
  deadset, venatic, wanlasour
HURT   see PAIN
HUSBAND   see MEN/WOMEN
IDEAS   see BELIEF(S) or CREATIVITY/NEWNESS
IDOLS   see RELIGION
IGNORANCE   see KNOWLEDGE/STUPIDITY
IGNORING   see INDIFFERENCE/OVERCONCERN
ILLNESS/HEALTHINESS   (see also BODY, FEELING[S],
      HAPPINESS/UNHAPPINESS, MEDICINE, PAIN,
      WOUNDS)
  fastigium, hygeiolatry, lysis, malinger, valetudinarianism
ILLOGIC   see REASON/ILLOGICALITY
ILLUSION   see DECEPTION
IMAGINATION   see CREATIVITY/NEWNESS or DE-
      CEPTION
IMITATION   see REPETITION/DUPLICATION
IMMUNITY   see FEELING(S)
IMPORTANCE/UNIMPORTANCE   (see also INDIF-
      FERENCE/OVERCONCERN, LARGENESS,

LENGTH, NEEDLES/PINS [AS IN IMPORTANT
POINTS], THINGS/REALITY, WEALTH/
POVERTY, WEIGHT)

acrolect, adoxography, banality, equiponderate, expeditio, fastigium, fleabite, foma, gravamen, hippopotomonstrosesquipedalian, knickknackatory, lilas, lubber-wort, microlipet, nosism, pismirism, poncif, pons asinorum, pro tanto, wegotism

IMPOSSIBILITY   see REASON/ILLOGICALITY

IMPURITY   see POISON

INABILITY   see ABILITY/INABILITY

INCOMPLETENESS   (see also FIRST/LAST,
SUCCESS/FAILURE)

catagraph, Zeigarnik effect

INCREASE   see NUMBERS

INDEPENDENCE   see DEPENDENCE/
INDEPENDENCE

INDIFFERENCE/OVERCONCERN   (see also FEARS,
IMPORTANCE/UNIMPORTANCE, LOVE/HATE,
SLEEP, STRICTNESS, THOUGHT, WANT, WILL-
POWER, COMPULSION/CONTROL, WORK)

adiaphoristic, anomy, beauism, blinkard, Cassandra, dishabille, erotomania, gongoozler, hygeiolatry, Micawberish, micrology, valetudinarianism, velleity

INFECTION   see POISON

INFERIORITY   see IMPORTANCE/UNIMPORTANCE

INFLEXIBILITY   see STRICTNESS

INFORMATION   (see also ARGUMENT, EVENTS,
KNOWLEDGE/STUPIDITY, MEMORY, NEWS,
OPEN/CLOSE [AS IN OPEN MIND],
QUESTION/ANSWER, SHOWS, SPEAKING)

confabulation, phatic, punctatim

INK   see WRITING

IN-LAWS   see FAMILY

INSECTS (see also ANIMALS, LARGENESS/
      SMALLNESS, NATURE)
  aculeate, formication, imago, instar
INSIGNIFICANCE see IMPORTANCE/
      UNIMPORTANCE
INSTRUCTION see KNOWLEDGE/STUPIDITY
INSTRUMENTS see MEASUREMENT or SOUND
INSULT see ARGUMENT
INTELLIGENCE see KNOWLEDGE/STUPIDITY
INTERCOURSE see SPEAKING or SEX
INTERPRETATION (see also WORDS)
  eisegesis, hermeneutics, oneirocritic
INTERRELATIONSHIP see CONNECTION/GAP/
      LOSS
INTRODUCTIONS see FIRST/LAST
ISLAND (see also LAND, ONE [AS IN ALONE],
      WATER)
  calf, holmgang
JOINING see CONNECTION/GAP/LOSS
JUMP see TURNING
KEYS see OPEN/CLOSE
KILLING see DEATH
KINDNESS see LOVE/HATE
KITCHEN see PLATES AND PANS
KNEES see BODY
KNIVES see CUTTING
KNOWLEDGE/STUPIDITY (see also ABILITY/
      INABILITY, ARGUMENT, BELIEFS,
      CAUSE/EFFECT, COVERING [AS IN CLOSED
      MIND], GROWTH/DEFORMITY, GUARANTEES/
      CERTAINTY, INFORMATION, INTERPRETA-
      TION, LIGHT/DARK, MEMORY, OPEN/CLOSE
      [AS IN OPEN MIND], PROBLEMS, QUESTION/

ANSWER, REASON/ILLOGICALITY, STRAT-
EGY, TESTS, THOUGHT, VISION)

acatalepsy, aporia, bellwether, charette, dysanagnosia,
fagin, hypnopedia, Kallikak, law of exercise, lucubration,
miscorrection, mucker pose, mumpsimus, omniscient,
pansophy, parachronism, paroemiology, pilpul, pons asinorum, Quinalpus, resipiscent, subaudition, tanquam,
udney, ultracrepidarianism

LACK   see WEALTH/POVERTY

LAND   (see also COUNTRY, DIRT/CLEANING,
EARTHQUAKES, GROWTH/DEFORMITY,
HOME, ISLAND, MOUNTAINS, NATURE,
SPACES, WORLD/EVERYTHING)

firebreak, latifundian, peneplain/peneplane, stalch, tri-
phibious, water-sick

LANGUAGE   see SPEAKING

LARGENESS/SMALLNESS   (see also FAT, HAIRS/
HAIRTHIN, IMPORTANCE/UNIMPORTANCE,
INSECTS [AS IN TINY CREATURES],
LENGTH/DEPTH, NUMBERS, WEALTH/
POVERTY)

Balkanize, calf, chiliagon, etui/etwee, fenestella/wicket,
hallux, jumboism, micrology, pugil, supercalendar

LAST   see FIRST

LAUGHTER   (see also HAPPINESS/UNHAPPINESS)
agelast, cachinnate

LAW   (see also CRIME, EQUALITY/FAIRNESS/BIAS,
GOVERNMENT, LEADERS/LEADERSHIP,
RULEMAKERS/RULE-FOLLOWERS)

anomy, civil death, dysnomy, insilium, misfeasance

LAZINESS   see TIREDNESS

LEADERS/LEADERSHIP   (see also DEPENDENCE/
INDEPENDENCE, DIRECTION, FIRST/LAST,

GOVERNMENT, RULE-MAKERS/RULE-
FOLLOWERS)

chirotony, doyen, empleomania, numen, roorback, Sherman statement

LEANING   see TURNING

LEARNING   see KNOWLEDGE/STUPIDITY

LEAVING   see OPEN/CLOSE

LEFT   see DIRECTION

LEGALITY   see LAW

LEGS   see BODY

LENGTH/DEPTH   (see also GOOD/BAD [AS IN
LOWNESS/EVIL], IMPORTANCE/
UNIMPORTANCE, LARGENESS/SMALLNESS,
MOUNTAINS, TIME, WATER)

bletonism, festination, hippopotomonstrosesquipedalian,
pro tanto, sesquipedalian, spindle

LETTERS   see WORDS or WRITING

LEVEL   see FLATNESS

LIBERTY   see EQUALITY/FAIRNESS/BIAS

LIES   see DECEPTION

LIFTING   see CARRYING

LIGHT/DARK   (see also COLORS, FEAR,
KNOWLEDGE/STUPIDITY, SHADOW, STARS,
SUN, VISION)

chiaroscuro, footcandle, heliotropic, lucubration, nyctalopia, pharology, phosphorescence, photobiotic, photolysis, photopathy, scotophobia, translucent

LIGHTNESS   see WEIGHT

LIKE   see LOVE/HATE

LIQUID   (see also ALCOHOL, CRYING, DROPS/
DROPPING/DRIPPING, FOOD, WATER)

sup, supernaculum

LIVING   see GROWTH/DEFORMITY

LOCATION   see SPACES

LOCKING   see OPEN/CLOSE
LOGIC   see REASON/ILLOGICALITY
LOOKING   see VISION
LOOSENESS   see STRENGTH/WEAKNESS
LOSING   see CONNECTION or SUCCESS/FAILURE
LOVE/HATE   (see also HEART, NICENESS, GIVING/
        TAKING, ARGUMENT, PRAISE, FRIENDS,
        FIGHTING, MARRIAGE, SEX, INDIFFERENCE/
        OVERCONCERN, EQUALITY/FAIRNESS/BIAS,
        HAPPINESS/UNHAPPINESS, GOOD/BAD)
   achthronym/ethnophaulism, ailurophile, ailurophobe, an-
   tiverbality, dyscalligynia, emulous, hippomaniac, ia-
   tromisia, jumboism, microlipet, misapodysis, misocainia,
   misocapnist, misogamist, mucker pose, oriflamme, scri-
   bacious, scunner, soceraphobia, teratism, tertius gaudens,
   udney, vade mecum
LOWNESS   see LENGTH/DEPTH
LUCK   (see also GAMBLING, STRATEGY, SUCCESS/
        FAILURE, WILLPOWER/COMPULSION/
        CONTROL)
   aleatory, serendipity
LUNCH   see FOOD
MACHINES   (see also THINGS/REALITY, WORK)
   immachination
MAGAZINES   see WORDS
MAKEUP   (see also BEAUTY, CHARACTER, COVER-
        ING, WRINKLES)
   fard, infucation
MALES   see MEN/WOMEN
MANURE   see WASTE
MAPS   (see also DIRECTION, STRATEGY, WORLD/
        EVERYTHING)
   Kriegspiel

MARRIAGE   (see also ONE [AS IN SINGLE], FAMILY, HOME, MEN/WOMEN, SEX)

anuptaphobia, benedict, cagamosis, deuterogamist, endogamy, exogamy, hereism, heterogamosis, nomogamosis, pseudogyny

MATCHBOXES   (see also COLD/NOT, FIRE, SMOKING)

cumyxaphily

MATCHED   see GOOD/BAD

MATERIAL WORLD   see THINGS/REALITY

MATHEMATICS   (see also MEASUREMENT, NUMBERS)

acalculia, surd

MEANING   see WORDS

MEASUREMENT   (see also MATH, NUMBERS, TESTS)

konimeter, nephometer, orometer, udometer

MEDICINE   (see also BODY, ILLNESS/HEALTHINESS, PAIN)

aegrotat, debridement, holagogue, iatrapistia, iatrogenic, iatromisia, iatrophobia, nosocomephobia, patellar reflex, thalassotherapy

MELTING   see COLD/HOT

MEMORY   (see also CONNECTION/GAP/LOSS, INFORMATION, KNOWLEDGE/STUPIDITY, THOUGHT)

confabulation, eidetic, gowyop, lacuna, law of recency, logamnesia, logamnosis, mnemonic, nepenthe, revenant, Zeigarnik effect

MEN/WOMEN   (see also ANIMALS, CHARACTER, CHILDREN, FAMILY, GROWTH/DEFORMITY, HOME, MARRIAGE, NATURE, SEX)

Adonis, anacampserote, anthropopithecus, dyscalligynia,

equalitarian, hindermate, kaleidogyn, misandry, pornogenarian, thelyphthoric

MESSY   see GOOD/BAD

METALS   (see also MINING)
  scissel

MILITARY   see WAR

MIMICKING   see REPETITION/DUPLICATION

MIND   see THOUGHT

MINING   (see also HUNTING, METALS, WANT [AS IN
      SEARCHING])
  mullock/tailing, stalch, stull

MINISTERS   see RELIGION

MISSING   see CONNECTION

MISTAKE   see KNOWLEDGE

MOBS   see CROWDS

MONEY   (see also DEBT, GAMBLING, GIVING/
      TAKING, WEALTH/POVERTY)
  agiotage, claqueur, desterilize, heredipety, instant/
  extra/quickie, mataeotechny, oniomania, pornopatch,
  quaestuary, rackrent, scissel, tertius gaudens, wergild

MONSTERS   see GOOD/BAD

MORALITY   see GOOD/BAD

MORNING   see TIME

MOTHER   see MEN/WOMEN

MOTION   see TURNING

MOUNTAINS   (see also COUNTRY, LAND,
      LENGTH/DEPTH, PROBLEMS, STONES)
  orogeny, orometer, scree

MOURNING   see DEATH

MOUTH   (see also FLAVOR, FOOD, OPEN/CLOSE,
      POKING/PRICKING . . . , SPEAKING, TASTE,
      WORDS)
  aboral, disgorger, sup

MOVEMENT   see TURNING

MOVIES   (see also DRAMA, STARS, VISION)
  noodling
MUSIC   see SOUND
MYTH   see KNOWLEDGE/STUPIDITY
NAMES   (see also WORDS)
  pseudogyny
NATION   see COUNTRY
NATURE   (see also ANIMALS, CHARACTER, COUN-
      TRY, LAND, MEN/WOMEN, ONE, PLANTS,
      SPACES, STARS, SUPERNATURAL, THINGS/
      REALITY, WORLD/EVERYTHING)
  anomy, photopathy, quiddity, stenotopic
NAVY   see WAR
NEARNESS   see CONNECTION/GAP/LOSS
NEEDLES/PINS   (see also HAIRS/HAIRTHIN, POKING/
      PRICKLING, YARN)
  aichmophobia, etui/etwee
NEIGHBORS   see FRIENDS/STRANGERS
NEST   see HOME
NET   see CONNECTION/GAP/LOSS
NEUTRALITY   see EQUALITY/FAIRNESS/BIAS
NEVER   see TIME
NEWNESS   see CREATIVITY/NEWNESS
NEWS   (see also EVENTS, INFORMATION)
  amblysia
NEWSPAPERS   see WORDS
NICENESS   (see also LOVE/HATE)
  asteism, gixlety, obsequiousness
NIGHT   see TIME
NIGHTMARES   see SLEEP
NOISE   see SOUND
NOSE   (see also BREATHING, FEELING[S], SMELL,
      SNEEZING)
  emunction, retroussé

NUDITY   see COVERING

NUMBERS   (see also AGE, CONNECTION/GAP/LOSS,
    DROPS/DROPPING/DRIPPING, FIRST/LAST,
    LARGENESS/SMALLNESS, MATH, MEASURE-
    MENT, ONE, THREE, TWO, WEALTH/
    POVERTY)
  fallacy of the beard, numerate

NUTRITION   see FOOD

OATH   see PROMISE

OBLIGATION   see WORK

OBSESSION   see INDIFFERENCE/OVERCONCERN

OCEAN   see WATER

ODDNESS   see DIFFERENTNESS/CHANGE/
    SAMENESS

ODOR   see SMELL

OFFICE   see WORK or LEADERS/LEADERSHIP

OLD AGE   see AGE

ONE   (see also CROWDS, FIRST/LAST, ISLAND [AS
    IN ALONE], MARRIAGE [AS IN SINGLE],
    NUMBERS, TWO)
  monepic, multivocal, quiddity, seriatim

OPEN/CLOSE/PERMITTING/PROHIBITING   (see also
    COVERING, CUTTING, DECEPTION, FOOD
    [AS IN SWALLOWING], GIVING/TAKING [AS
    IN REMOVAL], HUNTING [AS IN CAPTUR-
    ING], KNOWLEDGE/STUPIDITY [AS IN OPEN
    MIND], TRAVEL [AS IN ESCAPING], VISION)
  adfenestrate, aniconic, antephialtic, antipluvial, apotropaic, defenestrate, disembosom, disgorger, elapidation,
  erotodromomania, firebreak, holagogue, mullion,
  paragenital, passe-partout, peribolos, prescind, stridor,
  stull

OPINION   see THOUGHT

OPPOSITENESS   (see also ARGUMENT,

DIFFERENTNESS/CHANGE/SAMENESS,
FIGHTING, TURNING)
  antisyzygy, opposable, oxymoron
OPPOSITION   see FIGHTING
ORGANISMS   see NATURE
ORIGINS   see FIRST/LAST
OVERATTENTION   see
      INDIFFERENCE/OVERCONCERN
OVERCONCERN   see INDIFFERENCE/
      OVERCONCERN
OVERSIMPLIFICATION   see DECEPTION
OWNERSHIP   see WEALTH/POVERTY
OXYGEN   see AIR
PADDING   see DECEPTION
PAIN   (see also BODY, CONFESSION/
      FORGIVENESS/REMORSE, FEELING[S],
      FIGHTING, ILLNESS/HEALTHINESS,
      LOVE/HATE, MEDICINE, WOUNDS)
  fleabite, longanimity, nepenthe, travail
PAINTING(S)   (see also ART, PICTURES)
  craquelure
PARENTING   see FAMILY
PAYMENT   see MONEY
PEACE   (see also HAPPINESS/UNHAPPINESS,
      SOUND, WAR)
  modus vivendi, parley, Wanderjahr
PEOPLE   see MEN/WOMEN
PERCEPTIONS   see FEELING(S)
PERFECTION   see GOOD/BAD or STRICTNESS
PERMISSION   see OPEN/CLOSE
PERSUASION   see ARGUMENT
PHOBIAS   see FEARS
PHOTOGRAPHS   see PICTURES
PHRASES   see WORDS

PICKING see POKING/PRICKLING

PICTURES (see also ART, PAINTINGS, SYMBOLS, WORDS, WRITING)

aniconic, calcographer, daub, grangerize, iconolagny, Rorschach test

PIMPLES (see also BEAUTY, GROWTH/DEFORMITY, MAKEUP, SPOTS, WOUNDS, WRINKLES)

horripilation, phaneromania

PINS see NEEDLES/PINS

PITCH see SOUND

PLACES see WORLD/EVERYTHING

PLANS see STRATEGY

PLANTS (see also FOOD, GRAIN, GROWTH/ DEFORMITY, NATURE, WASTE, WOOD)

acetarious, calathus, deciduous, embower, halobios, interlucation, remontant, serotinous

PLATES AND PANS (see also FOOD, FLATNESS)

critouns, gowpen

PLAYING (see also STRATEGY)

dub/palooka, J'adoubovitz, necromimesis, pone, trey

PLAYS see DRAMA

PLEASURE see HAPPINESS/UNHAPPINESS

PLEDGE see PROMISE

POINTING see POKING/PRICKLING

POISON (see also DIRT/CLEANING, GOOD/BAD, SMOKING)

debridement, lurgulary, molysmophobia/mysophobia

POKING/PRICKLING/POINTING/BITING/PICKING (see also CUTTING, DIRECTION, FIGHTING, NEEDLES/PINS, SCRATCHING/TICKLING)

aculeate, banderilla, emunction, exoculate, peneplain/ peneplane, punctatim

POLITICS see LEADERS/LEADERSHIP

POPULARITY see CROWDS

POSITION   see DIRECTION or SPACES

POSSESSIONS   see THINGS/REALITY

POSSIBILITIES   see DIFFERENTNESS/CHANGE/
SAMENESS or LUCK

POVERTY   see WEALTH/POVERTY

PRACTICE   see REPETITION/DUPLICATION

PRAISE   (see also APPLAUSE, GIVING/TAKING,
SPEAKING)
  puff

PREACHING   see RELIGION

PRECISION   see STRICTNESS

PREJUDICE   see EQUALITY/FAIRNESS/BIAS

PREVENTION   see OPEN/CLOSE

PRICKING   see POKING/PRICKING

PRIDE   (see also LOVE/HATE)
  orgulous

PRIVATE   see SECRECY/SECRETS/SURPRISE

PRIZES   see GIVING/TAKING

PROBABILITY   see LUCK

PROBLEMS   (see also ABILITY/INABILITY, ARGU-
MENT, KNOWLEDGE/STUPIDITY, MOUN-
TAINS, QUESTION/ANSWER, STRATEGY,
THOUGHT)
  fallacy of the beard

PROCRASTINATION   (see also TIME)
  blinkard, cunctatious

PRODUCTIVITY   see WORK

PROHIBITING   see OPEN/CLOSE

PROMISE · (see also CONFESSION/FORGIVENESS/
REMORSE, DECEPTION)
  admanuensis

PRONUNCIATION   see SPEAKING

PROOF   see ARGUMENT

PROPERTY   see THINGS/REALITY

PROSTITUTION   see SEX
PROTECTING   see OPEN/CLOSE
PUNISHMENT   (see also CONFESSION/FORGIVE-
      NESS/REMORSE, DEATH, FIGHTING,
      WARNING[S]/THREAT[S])
  longanimity
PURE   see CUTTING (AS IN UNCUT)
PURPOSE   see REASON/ILLOGICALITY
PURSUIT   see HUNTING
PUZZLES   see PLAYING
QUALIFIED   see ABILITY/INABILITY
QUANTITY   see NUMBERS
QUESTION/ANSWER   (see also ARGUMENT,
      KNOWLEDGE/STUPIDITY, PROBLEMS,
      REASON/ILLOGICALITY, STRATEGY,
      TESTS, WORDS)
  anacoenosis, erotetic/pysmatic, insilium, sermocination,
  sockdolager, ultracrepidarianism
RACE   see SKIN or COLORS
RADIO   see SHOWS
RAGGED   see GOOD/BAD
RAIN   (see also DROPS/DROPPING/DRIPPING, LIQ-
      UID, WATER)
  spit, udometer
RANK   see LEADERS/LEADERSHIP
READING   (see also VISION, WORDS, WRITING)
  alexia, numerate, omnilegent
REALITY   see THINGS/REALITY
REASON/ILLOGICALITY   (see also ARGUMENT, BE-
      LIEFS, CAUSE, COVERING [AS IN OPEN
      MIND], DECEPTION, KNOWLEDGE/
      STUPIDITY, OPEN/CLOSE [AS IN OPEN
      MIND], PROBLEMS, QUESTION/ANSWER,
      STRATEGY, THOUGHT)

anachorism, euhemerism, nympholepsy, scunner, syncretism

RECIPES   see FOOD

RECORDS   (see also SOUND)

discophily

REFLEX   (see also TURNING, WILLPOWER/
    COMPULSION/CONTROL)

patellar reflex

RELATEDNESS   see CONNECTION/GAP/LOSS

RELATIVES   see FAMILY

RELIGION   (see also BELIEFS, CONFESSION/
    FORGIVENESS/REMORSE, GOOD/BAD, HELL,
    LOVE/HATE, SUPERNATURAL)

adiaphoristic, admanuensis, aniconic, antinomian, aseity,
eisegesis, hagiarchy, henotheism, hermeneutics, hieromachy, lilas, peribolos, pilpul, sabaist, solifidian, tergiversation, theomachist

REMORSE   see CONFESSION/FORGIVENESS/
    REMORSE

REMOVAL   see OPEN/CLOSE

REPETITION/DUPLICATION   (see also RETURNING,
    SUBSTITUTION, TWO, WORK)

battologist, doppelgänger, dun, exemplar, law of exercise,
penelopize, psellismophobia, scofflaw

REPLY   see QUESTION/ANSWER

REPRESSION   see OPEN/CLOSE

REPUTATION   (see also GOOD/BAD, LOVE/HATE)

roorback

REQUESTS   see QUESTION/ANSWER

RESIDENCE   see HOME

RESIGNATION/GIVING UP   (see also CONFESSION/
    FORGIVENESS/REMORSE)

resupination, tergiversation

RESPECT   see LOVE/HATE

RESPONSE   see QUESTION/ANSWER

RESPONSIBILITY   see WORK

RESTRICTION   see LAW or OPEN/CLOSE

RESULTS   see CAUSE/EFFECT

RETURNING   (see also REPETITION/DUPLICATION,
     TRAVEL, TURNING)
  anabiosis, anacampserote, instauration, revenant

REVENGE   see PUNISHMENT

REVERSAL   see TURNING

REWARD   see MONEY or PRAISE

RHYTHM   see TIME or SOUND

RICHNESS   see WEALTH/POVERTY

RIDGE   see WRINKLES

RIGHT   see DIRECTION

RIGHTS   see EQUALITY/FAIRNESS/BIAS

RINGING   see SOUND

ROADS   (see also TRAVEL, WHEELS)
  hodophobia

ROCKS   see STONES

RODS   (see also HAIRS/HAIRTHIN, LENGTH/DEPTH,
     NEEDLES/PINS)
  mullion

ROLLING   see TURNING

ROMANCE   see LOVE/HATE

ROPE   see HAIRS/HAIRTHIN

ROUND   see WHEEL

RUBBING   see HANDS

RULEMAKERS/RULE-FOLLOWERS   (see also BE-
     LIEF[S], DEBT, GOVERNMENT, LAW,
     LEADERS/LEADERSHIP, STRICTNESS, WORK)
  bellwether, Moloch, obsequiousness, supererogate

RUNNING   (see also DANCING, FEET, OPEN/CLOSE
     [AS IN ESCAPING], TRAVEL, WALKING)
  absquatulate

SACRIFICE   see GIVING/TAKING
SADNESS   see HAPPINESS/UNHAPPINESS
SAILING   see SHIPS
SALADS   see FOOD
SALE   see MONEY
SAMENESS   see DIFFERENTNESS/CHANGE/
        SAMENESS
SAND   (see also DIRT/CLEANING, STONES, WATER)
   struthionine
SATISFACTION   see HAPPINESS/UNHAPPINESS
SAVING   see WASTE or MONEY
SAWING   see CUTTING
SCABS   see WOUNDS
SCARCITY   see NUMBERS
SCIENCE   (see also KNOWLEDGE/STUPIDITY, MA-
        CHINES)
   mataeotechny
SCRATCHING/TICKLING   (see also CUTTING, FEEL-
        ING[S], HANDS, POKING/PRICKING . . . ,
        WOUNDS)
   rasorial
SEALS   see SYMBOLS
SEARCHING   see VISION
SEASONS   see TIME
SECRECY/SECRETS/SURPRISE   (see also DECEP-
        TION, OPEN/CLOSE)
   absquatulate, deus ex machina, subdititious
SEEING   see VISION
SELF-DECEPTION   see DECEPTION
SELFISHNESS   see GIVING/TAKING
SELF-SUFFICIENCY   see DEPENDENCE/
        INDEPENDENCE
SELLING   see MONEY
SENSE   see KNOWLEDGE/STUPIDITY

SENSES   see FEELING(S)

SERIOUSNESS   see IMPORTANCE/UNIMPORTANCE

SERMONS   see RELIGION

SEX   (see also BODY, CONNECTION/GAP/LOSS,
      CREATIVITY/NEWNESS, DIRT/CLEANING,
      FAMILY, MARRIAGE, MEN/WOMEN)
   erotodromomania, erotomania, iconolagny, mazotropism,
   obsidium, penultima, philemyosis, pornopatch, pudendojacosis

SHADOW   (see also COVERING, DECEPTION, LIGHT/
      DARK, SUN)
   ascian

SHAKING   see EARTHQUAKES

SHARING   see GIVING/TAKING

SHARP   see POKING/PRICKING

SHAVING   see CUTTING

SHELLS   (see also BONES, COVERING, STONES,
      STRENGTH/WEAKNESS [AS IN HARDNESS])
   conchology

SHIPS   (see also TRAVEL, WAR, WATER)
   naufragous, naumachy, orthodromics, pharology, tack,
   thalassotherapy, velivolant, waveson

SHOOTING   see FIGHTING

SHORTNESS   see LENGTH/DEPTH

SHOWS   (see also APPLAUSE, AUDIENCE, EVENTS,
      INFORMATION)
   claqueur, quonking, tutti

SIBLINGS   see FAMILY

SICKNESS   see ILLNESS/HEALTHINESS

SIDES   (see also DIRECTION)
   anopisthographic, chiliagon

SIGHT   see VISION

SILENCE   see SOUND

SIMILARITY   see DIFFERENTNESS/CHANGE/
       SAMENESS
SIN   see GOOD/BAD
SINGLE   see MARRIAGE (AS IN UNMARRIED)
SISTERS   see FAMILY
SIZE   see LARGENESS/SMALLNESS
SKILL   see ABILITY/INABILITY
SKIN   (see also BEAUTY, BODY, FEELING[S],
       MAKEUP, PIMPLES, SEX, WOUNDS,
       WRINKLES)
   achthronym/ethnophaulism, chromatocracy, despumate
SKY   see AIR
SLEEP   (see also GOOD/BAD [AS IN NIGHTMARES],
       INDIFFERENCE/OVERCONCERN, TIREDNESS,
       WANT [AS IN DREAMS], WORK)
   antephialtic, clinophobia, decubitus, dereism, hypnope-
   dia, lychnobite, malneirophrenia, matutolypea, oneiro-
   critic, resupination
SLIPPERINESS   see CARRYING
SLOWNESS   see SPEED
SMALLNESS   see LARGENESS/SMALLNESS
SMELL(S)   (see also AIR, BREATHING, FEELING[S],
       GOOD/BAD, NOSE)
   anosmia, kakidrosis, mundungus, podobromhidrosis,
   smell-feast, synesthesia, tragomaschalia
SMOKING   (see also AIR, FIRE, MATCHBOXES, POI-
       SON)
   misocapnist, nepheligenous
SMOOTHNESS   see FLATNESS or ABILITY/
       INABILITY
SNEEZING   (see also NOSE, THROWING)
   ptarmic
SNOBBISHNESS   see IMPORTANCE/
       UNIMPORTANCE

SOCIAL STATUS   see LEADERS/LEADERSHIP
SOLUTIONS   see KNOWLEDGE/STUPIDITY
SOUND   (see also AUDIENCE, FEELING[S], PEACE,
    RECORDS)
  acouasm, asonia, cachinnate, cacophonophilist, latrability, lirp, longanimity, microphonia, noodling, onomatophobia, onomatopoeic, phonaesthesia, quonking, stridor,
  synesthesia, tutti, yaffling
SPACE(S)   (see also BUILDINGS, COUNTRY, LAND,
    NATURE, WORLD/EVERYTHING)
  cowcat, latebricole, Lebensraum
SPEAKING   (see also ARGUMENT, CONFESSION/
    FORGIVENESS/REMORSE, DECEPTION, IN-
    FORMATION, PRAISE, SOUND, THROAT,
    WORDS, WRITING)
  achthronym/ethnophaulism, acrolect, alalia/aphasia, amblysia, antapology, antiverbality, aporia, aposiopesis, banality, battologist, disembosom, dun, exordium, gam,
  hwyl, hyperurbanism, illeism, microphonia, nosism, patavinity, prolegomena, psellismophobia, screed, soliloquial,
  subarticulation, subaudition, ultracrepidarianism, wegotism, xenoglossia
SPEED   (see also DIFFERENTNESS/CHANGE/
    SAMENESS, DIRECTION, TIME, TRAVEL)
  absquatulate, bradyauxesis, bradycardia, bradytelic, expeditio, festination, ictal emotions, instant/extra/quickie,
  jarovize, lotic, saccade, sermocination, tachytelic
SPELLING   see WORDS
SPEWING   see THROWING
SPLITTING   see CUTTING
SPOILED   see WANT
SPOTS   (see also PIMPLES)
  trey
SPREADING   see COVERING

STAGE   see DRAMA
STAMPS   see SYMBOLS
STANDING   (see also CRAWLING, FEET, RUNNING,
    WALKING)
  birl
STARS   (see also AIR, LIGHT/DARK, MOVIES,
    NATURE, SUCCESS, SUN, WORLD/
    EVERYTHING)
  instar, querent, sabaist, sidereal, stellification
STATUS   see LEADERS/LEADERSHIP
STEALING   see GIVING/TAKING
STIMULATION   see FEELING(S)
STING   see POKING/PRICKING . . .
STOCKS   see MONEY
STONES   (see also ABSTRACT/CONCRETE, BUILD-
    INGS, MOUNTAINS, SAND, SHELLS,
    STRENGTH/WEAKNESS [AS IN HARDNESS],
    STRICTNESS [AS IN HARDNESS])
  elapidation, ossify, trig
STOPPAGE   see OPEN/CLOSE
STRAIGHTNESS   see DIRECTION or GOOD/BAD
STRANGERS   see FRIENDS/STRANGERS
STRATEGY   (see also LUCK, MAPS, PLAYING,
    QUESTION/ANSWER, REASON/ILLOGICALITY,
    SUCCESS/FAILURE, TESTS, TRAVEL [AS IN
    PURSUIT], WANT, WILLPOWER/COMPUC-
    SION/CONTROL)
  deus ex machina, hippodamist, hypobulia, immachina-
  tion, Kriegspiel, Micawberish, psaphonic, reify, trilemma,
  velleity
STREETS   see ROADS
STRENGTH/WEAKNESS   (see also ILLNESS/
    HEALTHINESS, IMPORTANCE/UNIMPOR-

TANCE, LARGENESS/SMALLNESS, SHELLS
[AS IN HARDNESS], TIREDNESS)

abulia, Balkanize, bellipotent, caducity, isocracy, microphonia, pollard

STRICTNESS (see also BELIEF[S], INDIFFERENCE/
OVERCONCERN, NEEDLES/PINS [AS IN
POINTED, DIRECT, PRECISE], RULE-MAKERS/
RULE-FOLLOWERS, STONES [AS IN HARD/
UNCHANGING])

pilpul

STRING see YARN

STUDENTS see KNOWLEDGE/STUPIDITY

STUPIDITY see KNOWLEDGE/STUPIDITY

SUBSTITUTION (see also DIFFERENTNESS/
CHANGE/SAMENESS, REPETITION/
DUPLICATION)

ersatz, subdititious

SUCCESS/FAILURE (see also ARGUMENT, DEATH,
DIRECTION, FIGHTING, FIRST/LAST,
GROWTH/DEFORMITY, LUCK, STARS [AS IN
FAME], WAR [AS IN WINNING A WAR],
WEALTH/POVERTY)

Cassandra, hindermate, kakorrhaphiophobia, martingale,
psaphonic, Quinapalus

SUGAR see FOOD

SUICIDE see DEATH

SUITABILITY see GOOD/BAD

SUITS see LAW

SUN (see also AIR, COLD/HOT, COLORS, COVER-
ING, FIRE, LIGHT/DARK, STARS, VISION)

insolate, tanling

SUPERNATURAL (see also BELIEFS, NATURE, RELI-
GION)

banshee, doppelgänger, eidolism, Kachina, numen, thaumaturgy, transvection

SURGERY   see MEDICINE

SURPRISE   see SECRECY/SECRETS/SURPRISE

SWIMMING   see WATER

SWITCHING   see SUBSTITUTION

SYMBOLS   (see also ART, PICTURES, WORDS)
calathus, obelize/athetize, oriflamme, pharology

TAKING   see GIVING/TAKING

TALKING   see SPEAKING

TALLNESS   see LENGTH/DEPTH

TASTE   (see also FEELING[S], FLAVOR, FOOD,
MOUTH)
ageusia, brackish

TEARING   see CUTTING

TEARS   see CRYING

TEETH   see MOUTH

TELEVISION   see SHOWS

TESTS   (see also KNOWLEDGE/STUPIDITY, MEA-
SUREMENT, PROBLEMS, QUESTION/ANSWER,
REASON/ILLOGICALITY
optotype, pons asinorum, Rorschach

THANKS   see PRAISE

THEATER   see DRAMA

THEFT   see GIVING/TAKING

THEOLOGY   see RELIGION

THEORIES   see BELIEF(S)

THINGS/REALITY   (see also IMPORTANCE/
UNIMPORTANCE, NATURE, ONE,
WEALTH/POVERTY, WORLD/EVERYTHING)
backberend, desterilize, eidolon, euhemerism, knickknackatory, oneirataxia, oniomania, solipsism, waveson

THINNESS   see HAIRS/HAIR-THIN or
LARGENESS/SMALLNESS

THOUGHT   (see also ARGUMENT, BELIEF[S], COVERING [AS IN OPEN MIND], DIRECTION, FEELING[S], HEAD, INDIFFERENCE/ OVERCONCERN, KNOWLEDGE/STUPIDITY, MEMORY, OPEN/CLOSE [AS IN OPEN MIND], PROBLEMS, QUESTION/ANSWER, REASON/ ILLOGICALITY, SPEED, STRATEGY)

aprosexia, congeries, prescind

THREAD   see YARN

THREATS   see WARNING(S)/THREAT(S)

THREE   (see also NUMBERS)

tertius gaudens, trey, trilemma

THROAT   (see also BODY, SPEAKING)

gorget

THOWING   (see also DIRECTION, FIGHTING, SNEEZING, TRAVEL)

defenestration

THUNDER   see SOUND

TICKLING   see SCRATCHING/TICKLING

TILTING   see TURNING

TIME   (see also AGE, CAUSE/EFFECT, CONNECTION/GAP/LOSS, EVENTS, FIRST/ LAST, LENGTH/DEPTH, MEMORY, NEWS, PROCRASTINATION, SPEED)

agelast, apaetesis, asymptotically, fastigium, gambler's fallacy, gongoozler, hesternopothia, law of recency, lucubration, lychnobite, macrophobia, matutine, nonce word, nyctalopia, paleomnesia, parachronism, penelopize, preagonal, prolegomena, remontant, revenant, screed, seriatim, spit, Wanderjahr

TIREDNESS   (see also SLEEP, STRENGTH/ WEAKNESS, WORK)

forfoughten, screed

TISSUES   (see also BODY)
debridement, syngenesiotransplantation
TOBACCO   see SMOKING
TOES   see FEET
TOMORROW   see TIME
TONGUE   see MOUTH
TOUCH   see FEELING(S)
TRACK   see HUNTING
TRAIL   see HUNTING
TRANSPORTATION   see TRAVEL
TRAPS   see OPEN/CLOSE
TRAVEL   (see also CARRYING, CRAWLING, DIREC-
      TION, DROPS/DROPPING/DRIPPING, FEET,
      OPEN/CLOSE [AS IN ESCAPING], RETURN-
      ING, ROADS, RUNNING, SHIPS, SPEED, STARS
      [AS FOR DIRECTIONS], STRATEGY [AS IN
      PURSUIT], VISITS, WALKING, WHEELS)
circumforaneous, enatation, erotodromomania, mundiva-
gant, revenant, spoor, transvection, vade mecum, Wan-
derjahr
TREES   see PLANTS
TRENDS   (see also CROWDS)
girouettism
TRICKERY   see DECEPTION
TRIVIA   see IMPORTANCE/UNIMPORTANCE
TRUTH   see REASON/ILLOGICALITY
TURNING   (see also DIFFERENTNESS/CHANGE/
      SAMENESS, DIRECTION, GROWTH/
      DEFORMITY, RETURNING)
ageotropic, anfractuous, bathos, birl, heliotropic, pudendojacosis, retroussé, resupination, saccade, supercalender, trig
TWISTING   see TURNING

TWO   (see also NUMBERS, REPETITION/
        DUPLICATION)
  bimester, binal, biunial, holmgang, martingale, sigmoidal
UGLY   see GOOD/BAD
UNCERTAINTY   see PROCRASTINATION
UNDERGROUND   see LENGTH/DEPTH
UNDRESSING   see COVERING
UNEXPECTEDNESS   see SECRECY/SECRETS/
        SURPRISE
UNHAPPINESS   see HAPPINESS
UNIMPORTANCE   see IMPORTANCE/
        UNIMPORTANCE
UNION   see CONNECTION/GAP/LOSS
UNIQUENESS   see ONE
UNIVERSE   see WORLD/EVERYTHING
UNKNOWN   see CONNECTION/GAP/LOSS or
        KNOWLEDGE/STUPIDITY
UNLOCKING   see OPEN/CLOSE
UNMARRIED   see MARRIAGE
UNORGANIZED   see GOOD/BAD
UPSIDE DOWN   see TURNING
VARIATION   see DIFFERENTNESS/CHANGE/
        SAMENESS
VEGETABLES   see PLANTS
VICTORY   see SUCCESS/FAILURE
VISION   (see also AUDIENCE, COLORS, COVERING,
        DECEPTION, EQUALITY/FAIRNESS/BIAS,
        FEELING[S], HUNTING, KNOWLEDGE/
        STUPIDITY, LIGHT/DARK, MOVIES,
        OPEN/CLOSE, READING, SECRECY/SECRETS/
        SURPRISE, SUN, WANT, WINDOWS)
  aceldama, achromatopsia/daltonism, agerasia, belvedere,
  blinkard, cryptoscopophilia, exoculate, gapeseed, gon-
  goozler, hemianopsia, mazotropism, optotype, prosopo-

lepsy, qualtagh, Rorschach test, saccade, scotoma, scotopia, synesthesia

VISIT   (see also TRAVEL)

   gam

VOICE   see SPEAKING

WAITING   see TIME

WALKING   (see also CRAWLING, FEET, RUNNING, STANDING, TRAVEL)

   cryptoscopophilia, equilibritist/schoenabatist, festination, flanerie, gressorial, oxter

WALLS   see OPEN/CLOSE

WANDERING   see TRAVEL

WANT   (see also INDIFFERENCE/OVERCONCERN, SLEEP [AS IN DREAMS], STRATEGY, TRAVEL [AS IN PURSUIT], WEALTH/POVERTY, WILLPOWER/COMPULSION/CONTROL, WORK)

   chimera, dereism, emulous, heredipety, hesternopathia, lilas, mammothrept, nympholepsy, oniomania, scripturient, tergiversation, velleity

WAR   (see also CRIME, DEATH, FIGHTING, PEACE, SHIPS, SUCCESS/FAILURE [AS IN WINNING A WAR], THROWING [AS IN EXPLOSIONS], WASTE)

   bellipotent, Kriegspiel

WARNING(S)/THREAT(S)   (see also ARGUMENT, FIGHTING, PUNISHMENT)

   Cassandra, pharology

WASTE   (see also DIRT/CLEANING, FOOD, GIVING/ TAKING, MONEY, WORK)

   cowcat, critouns, defenestration, encopresis, immerd, marasmic/marantic, mullock/tailing, saprophilous, scissel, scree, sideration, stercoration, voip

WATER   (see also AIR, CRYING, DROPS/DROPPING/

DRIPPING, FOOD, ISLAND, LAND, LENGTH/
DEPTH [AS IN OCEAN DEPTH], LIQUID, RAIN,
SHIPS)
  birl, bletonism, catadromous, enatation, enew, flotsam,
halobios, lotic, lurgulary, thalassotherapy, water-sick
WEAKNESS   see STRENGTH/WEAKNESS
WEALTH/POVERTY   (see also IMPORTANCE/
UNIMPORTANCE, MONEY, NUMBERS,
SUCCESS/FAILURE, THINGS/REALITY,
WANT [AS IN LACKING])
  latifundian, parvenu, plutocracy, ptochocracy, ptochogony
WEAPONS   see FIGHTING
WEB   see CONNECTION/GAP/LOSS
WEEK   see TIME
WEIGHT   (see also CARRYING, FAT [AS IN OVER-
WEIGHT], IMPORTANCE/UNIMPORTANCE,
LARGENESS/SMALLNESS)
  baragnosis
WHEELS   (see also ROADS, TRAVEL)
  trig
WHISPERING   see SPEAKING
WIDTH   see LENGTH/DEPTH
WIFE   see MEN/WOMEN
WILLPOWER/COMPULSION/CONTROL   (see also
ALCOHOL, INDIFFERENCE/OVERCONCERN,
REFLEX, WANT)
  abulia, encopresis, festination, immachination, Leben-
sraum, oniomania, opsomania, padrone, querent, sidereal,
tarantism, xenoglossia
WIND   see AIR
WINDOWS   (see also OPEN/CLOSE, VISION)
  cryptoscopophilia,   defenestration,   fenestella/wicket,
fenestral, fenestrated, mullion, roundel
WINNING   see SUCCESS/FAILURE

WINTER   see TIME
WISDOM   see KNOWLEDGE/STUPIDITY
WISHES   see WANT
WITCHES   see SUPERNATURAL
WOMEN   see MEN/WOMEN
WOOD   (see also NATURE, PLANTS)
  birl, rived, xylophilous
WORDS   (see also ARGUMENT, FEELING[S], INFOR-
      MATION, INTERPRETATION, NAMES, QUES-
      TION/ANSWER, READING, SPEAKING, SYM-
      BOLS, WRITING)
  dysanagnosia, grangerize, hadeharia, hippopotomonstrosesquipedalian, instant/extra/quickie, logamnesia,
  logamnosis, logophagist, managed text, monepic, *mot
  propre*, multivocal, multivocality, neologism, nonce
  word, obelize/athetize, onomatophobia, onomatopoeic,
  orismology, paradigmatic, pasilaly, phonaesthesia, poncif, pornopatch, prosopography, sesquipedalian, Sherman
  statement, signpost writing, syllabatim, syntagmatic, ultima, vade mecum
WORK   (see also CREATIVITY/NEWNESS,
      INDIFFERENCE/OVERCONCERN, REPETITION,
      RULE-MAKERS/RULE-FOLLOWERS, SLEEP,
      TIREDNESS, WANT, WASTE, WILLPOWER/
      COMPULSION/CONTROL)
  cafard, charette, hypengyophobia, lychnobite, malinger,
  Micawberish, padrone, paralipophobia, supererogate
WORLD/EVERYTHING   (see also ANIMALS, COUN-
      TRY, LAND, MEN/WOMEN, NATURE, ONE,
      PLANTS, SPACES, STARS, SUPERNATURAL,
      THINGS/REALITY)
  blabagogy, holagogue, mundivagant, omnilegent, omniscient, omnivorous, pansophy, pasilaly, passe-partout,
  phenotype, tutti, ubiquitous, vade mecum, Weltschmerz

WORRY   see FEARS

WORSHIP   see LOVE/HATE or RELIGION

WORTH   see IMPORTANCE/UNIMPORTANCE

WOUNDS   (see also FIGHTING, POKING/
        PRICKING . . . , PROBLEMS, SCRATCHING/
        TICKLING, WRINKLES)
  debridement, phaneromia

WRECKS   (see also GOOD/BAD, TRAVEL)
  flotsam, naufragous, waveson

WRESTLING   see FIGHTING

WRINKLES   (see also AGE, GROWTH/DEFORMITY,
        MAKEUP, PIMPLES, PROBLEMS, WOUNDS)
  dendrochronology, rhytiphobia, rhytiscopia, whorl

WRITING   (see also ART, PICTURES, READING,
        SPEAKING, SYMBOLS, WORDS)
  adoxography, anopisthographic, apostil, cacographer, calligraphy, catagraph, roorback, scribacious, scripturient

YARN   (see also DECEPTION [AS IN TALL TALE],
        HAIRS/HAIR-THIN, NEEDLES/PINS)
  filipendulous

YESTERDAY   see TIME

YOUNG   see AGE or CHILDREN